728.6 F2292   MAY   2006

Farmhouse

MID-CONTINENT PUBLIC LIBRARY
North Oak Branch
8700 N. Oak Trafficway   NO
Kansas City, MO 64155

WITHDRAWN NO
FROM THE RECORDS OF THE
MID-CONTINENT PUBLIC LIBRARY

The American Collection
FARMHOUSE

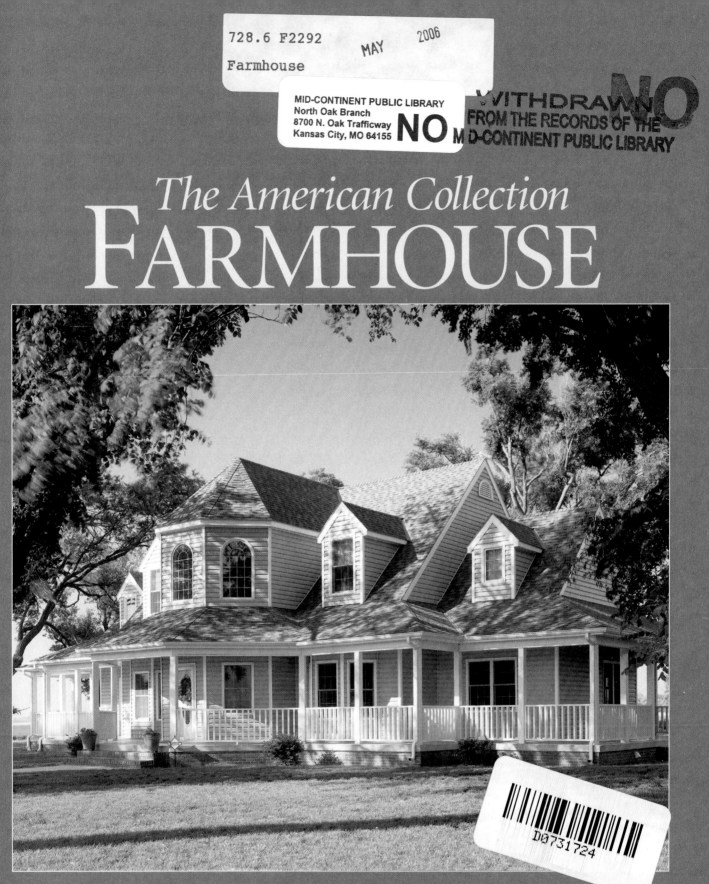

165 Home Plans with Country Style

Features Porches, Dormers, and Open Floor Plans

D0731724

The American Collection:
FARMHOUSE

6

Published by Hanley Wood
One Thomas Circle, NW, Suite 600
Washington, DC 20005

Distribution Center
PBD
Hanley Wood Consumer Group
3280 Summit Ridge Parkway
Duluth, Georgia 30096

Group Publisher, Andrew Schultz
Associate Publisher, Editorial Development, Jennifer Pearce
Managing Editor, Hannah McCann
Editor, Simon Hyoun
Assistant Editor, Kimberly Johnson
Publications Manager, Brian Haefs
Production Manager, Melissa Curry
Senior Plan Merchandiser, Nicole Phipps
Plan Merchandiser, Hillary Huff
Graphic Artist, Joong Min
Plan Data Team Leader, Susan Jasmin
Senior Marketing Manager, Holly Miller
Marketing Manager, Bridgit Kearns

National Sales Manager, Bruce Holmes

Most Hanley Wood titles are available at quantity discounts with bulk purchases for educational, business, or sales promotional use. For information, please contact Bruce Holmes at bholmes@hanleywood.com.

BIG DESIGNS, INC.
President, Creative Director, Anthony D'Elia
Vice President, Business Manager, Megan D'Elia
Vice President, Design Director, Chris Bonavita
Editorial Director, John Roach
Assistant Editor, Carrie Atkinson
Senior Art Director, Stephen Reinfurt
Production Director, David Barbella
Photo Editor, Christine DiVuolo
Graphic Designer, Frank Augugliaro
Graphic Designer, Billy Doremus
Graphic Designer, Jacque Young
Assistant Production Manager, Rich Fuentes

PHOTO CREDITS
Front Cover: Design HPK1900131 by Home Planners, Inc. For details, see page 141. Photo by Home Planners, Inc. Back Cover and Inset: Design HPK1900001 by Drummond Designs, Inc.
For details, see page 6. Photo by Drummond Designs, Inc.

10 9 8 7 6 5 4 3 2 1

All floor plans and elevations copyright by the individual designers and may not be reproduced by any means without permission. All text, designs, and illustrative material copyright ©2006 by Home Planners, LLC, wholly owned by Hanley-Wood, LLC. All rights reserved. No part of this publication may be reproduced in any form or by any means — electronic, mechanical, photomechanical, recorded, or otherwise — without the prior written permission of the publisher.

Printed in the United States of America

Library of Congress Control Number: 2005938830

ISBN-13: 978-1-931131-55-1
ISBN-10: 1-931131-55-4

MID-CONTINENT PUBLIC LIBRARY - QU

3 0003 00039460 9

MID-CONTINENT PUBLIC LIBRARY
North Oak Branch
8700 N. Oak Trafficway   NO
Kansas City, MO 64155

6

8

Contents

ONLINE EXTRA!

Hanley Wood Passageway

The Hanley Wood Passageway is an online
search tool for your home plan needs!
Discover even more useful information about
building your new home, search additional
new home plans, access online ordering, and
more at www.hanleywoodbooks.com/
acfarmhouse

hanley▲wood

FARMHOUSE STYLE

The classic shape and style of the American farmhouse is immediately recognizable. Whether glimpsed from the car window on a long country drive or captured in the background of Grant Wood's famous painting, farmhouses enhance the nation's landscape and inform the people's idea of home. Among the 165 homes collected in this book you'll find the same warmth and love of simple living that gave rise to the farmhouse style. And if you're looking to build your own farmhouse, remember that the blueprints for every home featured in this book are available for purchase. Find out more about buying home plans and blueprint packages on page 184, or visit www.eplans.com.

A wide front porch and traditional, two-story elevation make this home feel exactly right. See more of this design on page 80.

PHOTO COURTESY OF STEPHEN FULLER, INC.

From the outside, this family home's Victorian influence is apparent. Turn to page 84 to see what's inside.

PHOTO BY ANDREW D. LAUTMAN

USING THIS BOOK

Turn the page to take a tour of two finished homes that embody the farmhouse style. Then, beginning on page 11, is the Capes and Cottages section. Distinct and familiar, this architectural style began to take shape along the New England coast during the Colonial Revival period and gained popularity during the Depression. As then, economy of construction and low maintenance keep the small farmhouse a popular choice.

The Classic Farmhouses section begins on page 77. The two-story farmhouse dates back to the Victorian era, but current designs evolved to include elements from many architectural styles. Greek Revival details appear in the columns along the front porch, and widow's walks and romantic balconies originate in the Colonial styles of southern plantations. Many plans in this section include the convenience of a downstairs master bedroom, which makes the home a worthwhile investment that will endure for many years.

Finally, discover how contemporary amenities can complement traditional elegance. The homes collected in the Country Estates section (page 155) are modern variations of the estate homes built by wealthy landowners of the late 1800s.

Back then, Queen Anne designs and high European styles were the advantages of wealth, as are the spacious His and Hers walk-in closets, pampering first-floor master suites, and family-friendly media rooms of today's estates.

MAKING IT RIGHT

Found a home that's almost perfect for your family? Remember that nearly all the plans available from this collection or on eplans.com can be customized at your request. Perhaps you'd like to convert a study into a second bedroom suite, or swap in a side-loading three-car garage for a front-loading two-car design. Purchase a consultation with our modification specialist to find out all the ways you can personalize your new home. Turn to page 186 to find out more about customization, or call us to make an appointment.

FIND MORE HOMES

The 165 plans hand-collected in this book are a small sample of the thousands of designs in our library. To see the rest, visit the Hanley Wood Passageway for this book—and all the others—at www.hanleywoodbooks.com. You can also browse related articles about home design and home building, and complete your plan purchase. ■

FRESH FARMHOUSE

A unique approach brings the look for the farm
to a narrow lot

The wraparound porch and the angled approaching walkway add a sense of depth to this narrow-lot home.

You don't need sprawling acres of land to capture the refreshing feel of a farmhouse. This design brings country style to a 50-foot-wide footprint that would fit just as well in town as it would on a dirt road.

The home delivers a floor plan that offers both a living room and a family room, but the open design ensures the living room won't be forgotten like the small front rooms in so many classic Colonials. Instead, this living room opens easily into both the dining room and kitchen, creating a comfortable, welcoming atmosphere. A small porch off the dining room adds to its charm.

PHOTO COURTESY OF DRUMMOND DESIGNS, INC.

The galley-style kitchen features a built-in breakfast table, with another small porch attached. Linked to the dining room and living room on one side and the family room on the other, the kitchen easily serves as the center of the home. The living room is large and comfortable, with a fireplace at the center and windows on three sides.

Elsewhere on the first floor you'll find a quiet home office with windows overlooking the front yard. It's situated right next to the front door—perfect for a home-based business that welcomes the occasional client. You'll also find a coat closet next to both of the entrances and a laundry/utility room near the two-car garage.

Upstairs the master bedroom is, fittingly, the largest room in the house, with plenty of space to relax. A corner walk-in closet and a spacious master bath with separate shower add to the suite.

Two additional bedrooms, each with a spacious closet, share a full bath. The upstairs hallway includes an overlook that's open to the family room and dining room below—and offers the perfect location to place a computer workstation or a relaxing reading chair surrounded by bookshelves. ■

FOR MORE DETAILED INFORMATION, PLEASE CHECK THE FLOOR PLANS CAREFULLY.

FIRST FLOOR

SECOND FLOOR

plan# HPK1900001

First Floor: 1,274 sq. ft.
Second Floor: 1,009 sq. ft.
Total: 2,283 sq. ft.
Bedrooms: 3
Bathrooms: 2½
Width: 50' - 0"
Depth: 46' - 0"
Foundation: Unfinished Basement

ORDER ONLINE @ EPLANS.COM

THE RICHELIEU

The past comes to life in delightful fashion

Charming European details and dramatic rooflines distinguish the facade.

Exterior details convey the home's European influence: High-pitched roofs, decorative porch supports, and a stone facade are simply elegant elements from the French countryside. The interior prefers refinement, such as in the two-story foyer's graceful height and ornamental ceiling beams. With the nearby dining room and den, the spaces at the front of the plan offer a distinguished welcome to homeowners and guests. Beyond the foyer, the gathering room presents a comfortable compromise and transition between the formal spaces and the casual area encompassing the kitchen. The prominent fireplace occasions an attractive seating arrangement, while the open access to the dine-in kitchen and breakfast nook accommodate flexibility. The rear veranda is similarly versatile.

PHOTOS COURTESY OF LIVING CONCEPTS

Above: A tile backsplash is a good choice for the attractive, functional kitchen. Below: A handsome mantel and built-in cabinets complement the height of the gathering room.

Private spaces are uncommonly comfortable. The master suite features a spacious bath and walk-in closet, as well as direct access to the veranda. Even the second-floor bedrooms function as suites, easily sharing a com-partmented bath and the attractive overlook loft. Larger families should consider modifying either suite for more square footage. Finally, a detached above-garage suite provides for guests to this country manor. ■

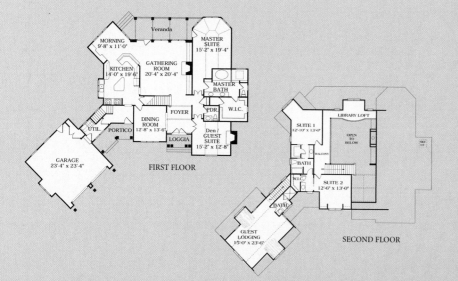

FIRST FLOOR

SECOND FLOOR

plan# HPK1900001

First Floor: 2,390 sq. ft.
Second Floor: 765 sq. ft.
Total: 3,155 sq. ft.
Bonus Space: 433 sq. ft.
Bedrooms: 4
Bathrooms: 3½
Width: 87' - 11"
Depth: 75' - 2"
Foundation: Crawlspace

ORDER ONLINE @ EPLANS.COM

Decorative ceiling treatments complement the Old-World look of the den. A front-facing window illuminates built-in details.

THIS HOME, AS SHOWN IN THE PHOTOGRAPHS, MAY DIFFER FROM THE ACTUAL BLUEPRINTS. FOR MORE DETAILED INFORMATION, PLEASE CHECK THE FLOOR PLANS CAREFULLY.

CAPES & COTTAGES

PHOTO COURTESY OF WILLIAM E. POOLE DESIGNS INC. - ISLANDS OF BEAUFORT, BEAUFORT, SC

Distinct and easily recognized, Cape Cod-style homes began to take shape along the New England coast during the Colonial Revival period. The designs were largely symmetrical and either one or one-and-a-half stories tall, which accommodated the harsh winter and gale-season weather experienced in the region. After its initial introduction in the 1700s, the style regained popularity during the Depression, when low construction cost was of the utmost importance and farming was the backbone of the nation's struggling economy. For many, these core values still hold true, and the small farmhouse continues to be a favorite.

The style may have originated along the Atlantic shores, but small embellishments make it suitable for any location. Shutters, once necessities against wind and rain, have withstood the test of time, only now as decorative accents. The long front porch with columns, not often seen in the original capes, is a design element borrowed from the Greek Revival styles of the colonial South. Today, it's difficult to imagine a farmhouse without a sprawling porch adorned with wooden rockers or a swing. The setting brings about images of chatting with neighbors in the twilight hours, or enjoying a glass of lemonade after a hard day working in the fields. Other Colonial elements, such as gabled roofs, also help define the style, while large front windows assure that a smaller home does not have to be a darker home.

The designs shown in the Capes and Cottages section represent a style of farmhouse architecture that has become a part of our nation's history and tradition. Whether nestled in the northeastern hills or stretching along a Midwestern countryside, these designs bring a touch of Americana to any neighborhood.

Flared eaves of the Dutch Colonial style distinguish this lovely design. See more of this plan on page 12.

PHOTO COURTESY OF: WILLIAM E. POOLE DESIGNS, INC. - ISLANDS OF BEAUFORT, BEAUFORT, SC.
THIS HOME AS SHOWN IN THE PHOTOGRAPH MAY DIFFER FROM THE ACTUAL BLUEPRINTS

Country flavor is well established on this fine three-bedroom home. The covered front porch welcomes friends and family alike to the foyer, where the formal dining room opens off to the left. The vaulted ceiling in the great room enhances the warmth of the fireplace and the wall of windows. An efficient kitchen works well with the bayed breakfast area. The secluded master suite offers a walk-in closet and a lavish bath; on the other side of the home, two family bedrooms share a full bath. Upstairs, an optional fourth bedroom is available for guests or in-laws and provides access to a large recreation room.

plan⊕# HPK1900003

Square Footage: 2,151
Bonus Space: 814 sq. ft.
Bedrooms: 3
Bathrooms: 2
Width: 61' - 0"
Depth: 55' - 8"
Foundation: Crawlspace, Unfinished Basement

ORDER ONLINE @ EPLANS.COM

ORDER BLUEPRINTS 24 HOURS, 7 DAYS A WEEK, AT 1-800-521-6797

THIS HOME, AS SHOWN IN THE PHOTOGRAPH, MAY DIFFER FROM THE ACTUAL BLUEPRINTS. FOR MORE DETAILED INFORMATION, PLEASE CHECK THE FLOOR PLANS CAREFULLY.

plan⊕ HPK1900004

First Floor: 1,651 sq. ft.
Second Floor: 567 sq. ft.
Total: 2,218 sq. ft.
Bedrooms: 3
Bathrooms: 2½
Width: 55' - 0"
Depth: 42' - 4"

ORDER ONLINE @ EPLANS.COM

A wonderful wraparound covered porch at the front and sides of this house and the open deck with a spa at the back provide plenty of outside living area. Inside, the spacious great room is appointed with a fireplace, cathedral ceiling, and clerestory with an arched window. The kitchen is centrally located for maximum flexibility in layout and features a food-preparation island for convenience. In addition to the master bedroom, with access to the sunroom, there are two second-level bedrooms that share a full bath.

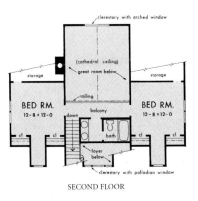

SECOND FLOOR

FIRST FLOOR

©1995 DONALD A. GARDNER ARCHITECTS, INC. PHOTOGRAPHY COURTESY OF DONALD A. GARDNER ARCHITECTS, INC. THE HOME AS SHOWN IN THE PHOTOGRAPH MAY DIFFER FROM THE ACTUAL BLUEPRINTS.

This charming country plan boasts a cathedral ceiling in the great room. Dormer windows shed light on the foyer, which opens to a front bedroom/study and to the formal dining room. The kitchen is completely open to the great room and features a stylish snack-bar island and a bay window in the breakfast nook. The master suite offers a tray ceiling and a skylit bath. Two secondary bedrooms share a full bath on the opposite side of the house. Bonus space over the garage may be developed in the future.

plan# HPK1900005

Square Footage: 1,832
Bonus Space: 425 sq. ft.
Bedrooms: 3
Bathrooms: 2
Width: 65' - 4"
Depth: 62' - 0"

ORDER ONLINE @ EPLANS.COM

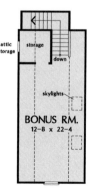

©1995 Donald A. Gardner Architects, Inc.

FIRST FLOOR

THIS HOME, AS SHOWN IN THE PHOTOGRAPH, MAY DIFFER FROM THE ACTUAL BLUEPRINTS. FOR MORE DETAILED INFORMATION, PLEASE CHECK THE FLOOR PLANS CAREFULLY.

plan# HPK1900006

Square Footage: 1,864
Bonus Space: 420 sq. ft.
Bedrooms: 3
Bathrooms: 2½
Width: 71' - 0"
Depth: 56' - 4"

ORDER ONLINE @ EPLANS.COM

REAR EXTERIOR

Quaint and cozy on the outside with porches front and back, this three-bedroom country home surprises with an open floor plan featuring a large great room with a cathedral ceiling. A central kitchen with an angled counter opens to the breakfast and great rooms for easy entertaining. The privately located master bedroom enjoys a cathedral ceiling and access to the deck. Two secondary bedrooms share a full hall bath. A bonus room makes expanding easy.

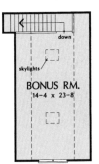

BONUS RM.
14-4 x 23-8

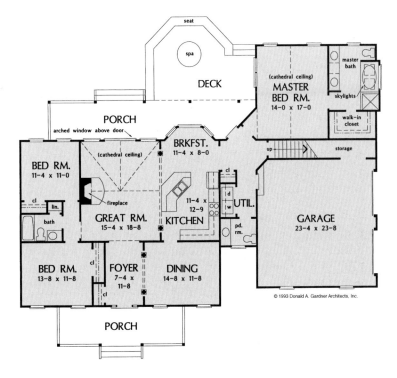

© 1993 Donald A. Gardner Architects, Inc.

©1995 DONALD A. GARDNER ARCHITECTS, INC. PHOTOGRAPHY COURTESY OF DONALD A. GARDNER ARCHITECTS, INC. THIS HOME AS SHOWN IN THE PHOTOGRAPH MAY DIFFER FROM THE ACTUAL BLUEPRINTS.

Dormers cast light and interest into the foyer for a grand first impression that sets the tone in this home full of today's amenities. The great room, articulated by columns, features a cathedral ceiling and is conveniently located adjacent to the breakfast room and kitchen. Tray ceilings and circle-top picture windows accent the front bedroom and dining room. A secluded master suite, highlighted by a tray ceiling in the bedroom, includes a bath with a skylight, a garden tub, a separate shower, a double-bowl vanity, and a spacious walk-in closet.

plan# HPK1900007

Square Footage: 1,879
Bonus Space: 360 sq. ft.
Bedrooms: 3
Bathrooms: 2
Width: 66' - 4"
Depth: 55' - 2"

ORDER ONLINE @ EPLANS.COM

REAR EXTERIOR

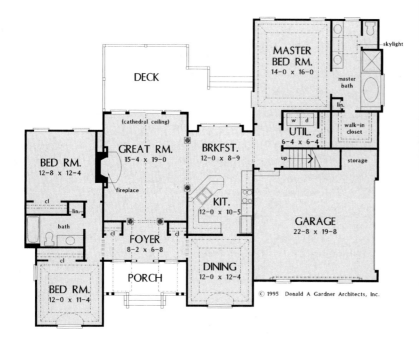

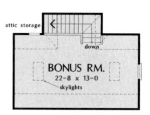

ORDER BLUEPRINTS 24 HOURS, 7 DAYS A WEEK, AT 1-800-521-6797

THIS HOME, AS SHOWN IN THE PHOTOGRAPH, MAY DIFFER FROM THE ACTUAL BLUEPRINTS. FOR MORE DETAILED INFORMATION, PLEASE CHECK THE FLOOR PLANS CAREFULLY.

plan# HPK1900008

Square Footage: 1,815
Bonus Space: 336 sq. ft.
Bedrooms: 3
Bathrooms: 2
Width: 70' - 8"
Depth: 70' - 2"

ORDER ONLINE @ EPLANS.COM

REAR EXTERIOR

Dormers, arched windows, and covered porches lend this home its country appeal. Inside, the foyer opens to the dining room on the right and leads through a columned entrance to the great room. The open kitchen easily serves the great room, the breakfast area, and the dining room. A cathedral ceiling graces the master suite, which is complete with a walk-in closet and a private bath. Two family bedrooms share a hall bath.

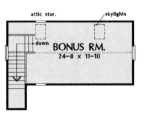

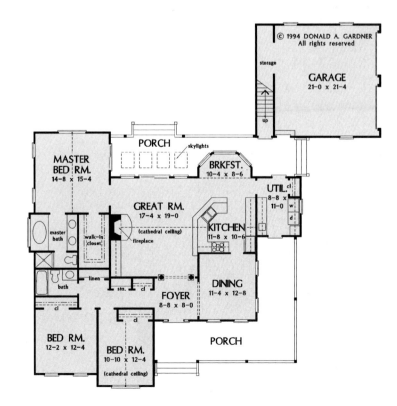

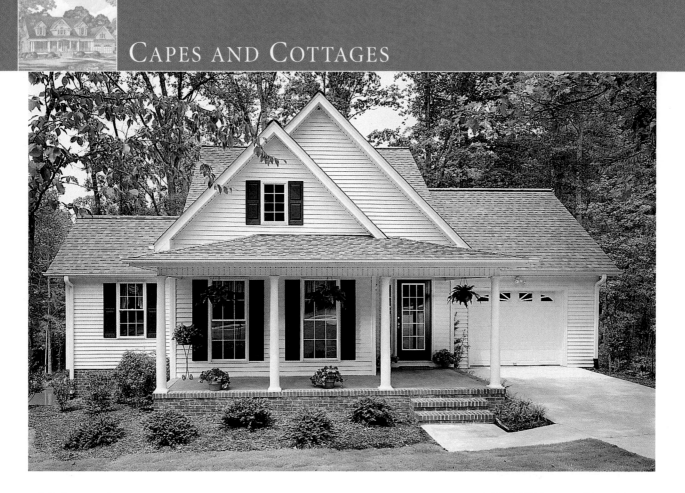

©1996 DONALD A. GARDNER ARCHITECTS, INC. PHOTOGRAPHY COURTESY OF DONALD A. GARDNER ARCHITECTS, INC.

This home is a great starter for a young family with plans to grow or for empty-nesters with a need for guest rooms. The two secondary bedrooms and shared bath on the second floor could also be used as office space. Additional attic storage is available as family needs expand. On the first floor, the front porch is perfect for relaxing. Inside, the foyer opens through a columned entrance to the large great room with its cathedral ceiling and fireplace. The master bedroom features a walk-in closet and a corner whirlpool tub.

plan # HPK1900009

First Floor: 1,116 sq. ft.
Second Floor: 442 sq. ft.
Total: 1,558 sq. ft.
Bedrooms: 3
Bathrooms: 2½
Width: 49' - 0"
Depth: 52' - 0"

ORDER ONLINE @ EPLANS.COM

FIRST FLOOR

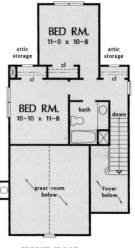

SECOND FLOOR

© 1994 Donald A. Gardner Architects, Inc.

THIS HOME, AS SHOWN IN THE PHOTOGRAPH, MAY DIFFER FROM THE ACTUAL BLUEPRINTS. FOR MORE DETAILED INFORMATION, PLEASE CHECK THE FLOOR PLANS CAREFULLY.

plan # HPK1900010

Square Footage: 1,787
Bonus Space: 326 sq. ft.
Bedrooms: 3
Bathrooms: 2
Width: 66' - 2"
Depth: 66' - 8"

ORDER ONLINE @ EPLANS.COM

REAR EXTERIOR

Cathedral ceilings bring a feeling of spaciousness to this home. The great room features a fireplace, cathedral ceilings, and built-in bookshelves. The kitchen is designed for efficient use with its food preparation island and pantry. The master suite provides a welcome retreat with a cathedral ceiling, a walk-in closet, and a luxurious bath. Two additional bedrooms, one with a walk-in closet, share a skylit bath. A second-floor bonus room is perfect for a future study or a play area.

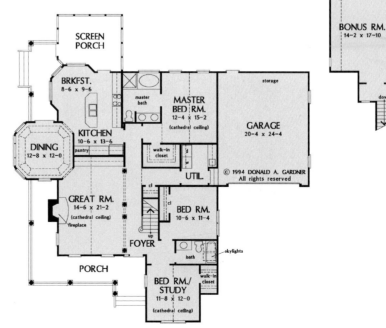

Craftsman-style windows decorate the facade of this beautiful bungalow design. Inside, the formal dining room, to the left of the foyer, can double as a study; the family room offers a sloping ceiling and a fireplace option. In the breakfast nook, a window seat and sliding glass doors that open to the covered patio allow homeowners to enjoy the outdoors. The master bedroom dominates the right side of the plan, boasting a walk-in closet and private bath. Upstairs, two secondary bedrooms—both with walk-in closets, and one with a private bath—sit to either side of a game room.

plan# HPK1900011

First Floor: 1,305 sq. ft.
Second Floor: 636 sq. ft.
Total: 1,941 sq. ft.
Bedrooms: 3
Bathrooms: 2½
Width: 42' - 4"
Depth: 46' - 10"
Foundation: Slab, Unfinished Basement, Crawlspace

ORDER ONLINE @ EPLANS.COM

FIRST FLOOR

SECOND FLOOR

plan# HPK1900012

First Floor: 1,050 sq. ft.

Second Floor: 458 sq. ft.

Total: 1,508 sq. ft.

Bedrooms: 3

Bathrooms: 2½

Width: 35' - 6"

Depth: 39' - 9"

Foundation: Pier (same as Piling)

ORDER ONLINE @ EPLANS.COM

This adorable abode could serve as a vacation cottage, guest house, starter home, or in-law quarters. The side-gabled design allows for a front porch with a "down-South" feel. Despite the small size, this home is packed with all the necessities. The first-floor master suite has a large bathroom and a walk-in closet. An open, functional floor plan includes a powder room, a kitchen/breakfast nook area, and a family room with a corner fireplace. Upstairs, two additional bedrooms share a bath. One could be used as a home office.

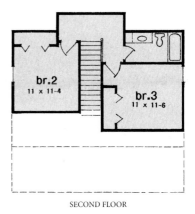

SECOND FLOOR

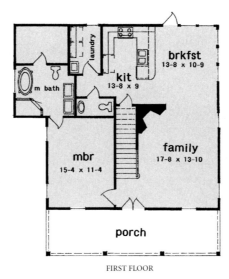

FIRST FLOOR

This massive ranch home offers a contemporary facade with a stone and siding combination. Wooden shutters around the windows offer a country flair. A large family room adjoins the kitchen and breakfast area with windows on two walls. The expansive foyer opens to the family room with a grand stone fireplace and open stairs to the basement. A private master bedroom suite features a raised tub in a bay window, a dramatic dressing area, and a huge walk-in closet.

plan# HPK1900013

Square Footage: 2,874
Bedrooms: 4
Bathrooms: 2½
Width: 83' - 0"
Depth: 50' - 4"
Foundation: Unfinished Basement

ORDER ONLINE @ EPLANS.COM

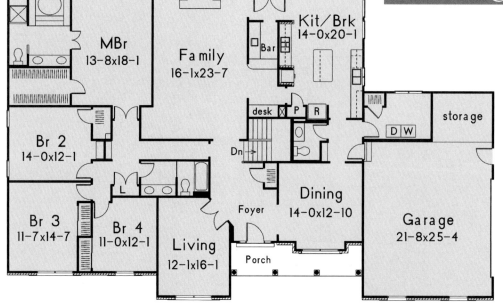

plan# HPK1900014

Square Footage: 1,366
Bedrooms: 3
Bathrooms: 2
Width: 71' - 4"
Depth: 35' - 10"
Foundation: Slab, Unfinished Basement, Crawlspace

ORDER ONLINE @ EPLANS.COM

A quiet, aesthetically pleasant, and comfortable one-story country home answers the requirements of modest-income families. The entrance to the house is sheltered by the front porch, which leads to the hearth-warmed living room. The master suite is arranged with a large dressing area that has a walk-in closet, plus two linear closets and space for a vanity. The main part of the bedroom contains a media center. The adjoining, fully equipped kitchen includes the dinette that can comfortably seat six people and leads to the rear terrace through six-foot sliding glass doors.

An eyebrow dormer and a large veranda give guests a warm country greeting outside; inside, vaulted ceilings lend a sense of spaciousness to this three-bedroom home. A bright country kitchen boasts an abundance of counter space and cupboards. The front entry is sheltered by a broad veranda. Built-in amenities adorn the interior, including a plant ledge over the entry coat closet, an art niche, a skylight, and a walk-in pantry and island workstation in the kitchen. A box-bay window and a spa-style tub highlight the master suite. The two-car garage provides a workshop area.

plan# HPK1900015

Square Footage: 1,408
Bedrooms: 3
Bathrooms: 2
Width: 70' - 0"
Depth: 34' - 0"
Foundation: Unfinished Basement, Crawlspace

ORDER ONLINE @ EPLANS.COM

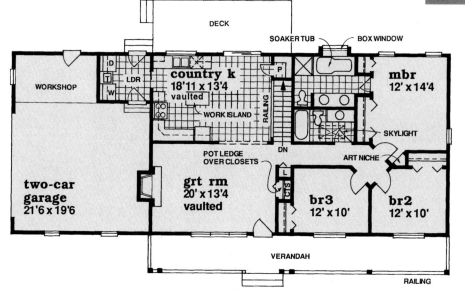

OPTIONAL LAYOUT

ORDER BLUEPRINTS 24 HOURS, 7 DAYS A WEEK, AT 1-800-521-6797

plan# HPK1900016

Square Footage: 1,820
Bonus Space: 470 sq. ft.
Bedrooms: 3
Bathrooms: 2
Width: 53' - 0"
Depth: 62' - 0"

ORDER ONLINE @ EPLANS.COM

This efficient design would suit a family just starting out as well as an empty-nester couple, providing all of the necessities, a few of the luxuries, and the opportunity to expand as needed. The principal living areas are arranged around the great room, where a cathedral ceiling and transom-topped windows visually expand the space. Built-in media cabinets and bookshelves flanking the fireplace lend a sense of formality and reduce furniture needs. The spacious island kitchen includes a computer center for conducting household business without leaving the hub of the home. In the front corner of the home, two bedrooms and a bath are perfect for children (or grandchildren). The master suite includes all the practical luxuries: dual sinks, compartmented bath, and large shower. If finished, the optional lower level provides over 1,000 square feet of recreational space for growing children or visiting family.

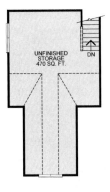

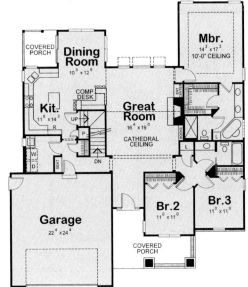

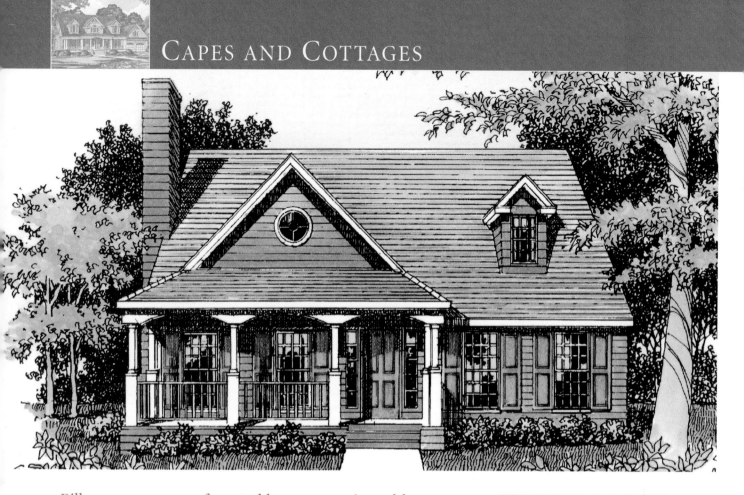

Pillars support a roof topped by an attractive gable, all covering the front porch of this fine three-bedroom home. Inside, the entrance opens directly to the great room, where a cathedral ceiling and a fireplace are enhancements. A gourmet kitchen offers a work island with a sink and serving counter for the nearby dining room. Located on the main level for privacy, the master bedroom is sure to please with two closets, one a walk-in, and a private bath with a separate tub and shower. Upstairs, two family bedrooms share a hall bath and access to a bonus room, perfect for a study or computer room.

plan# HPK1900017

First Floor: 1,216 sq. ft.
Second Floor: 478 sq. ft.
Total: 1,694 sq. ft.
Bonus Space: 115 sq. ft.
Bedrooms: 3
Bathrooms: 2½
Width: 38' - 0"
Depth: 38' - 8"
Foundation: Crawlspace, Unfinished Basement

ORDER ONLINE @ EPLANS.COM

Deck
38'-0" x 12'-0"

Kitchen
10'-0" x 14'-5"

Utility

Dining Rm.
10'-0" x 14'-5"

Pantry

Great Room
20'-0" x 16'-3"
(cathedral clg.)

Master Bedroom
13'-5" x 16'-3"

Porch
22'-8" x 6'-8"

FIRST FLOOR

Bedroom
14'-2" x 11'-10"

Bedroom
10'-1" x 11'-10"

Balcony

open to Great Room below

Bonus Rm.
13'-5" x 7'-2"

SECOND FLOOR

ORDER BLUEPRINTS 24 HOURS, 7 DAYS A WEEK, AT 1-800-521-6797

plan# HPK1900018

Square Footage: 1,484
Bedrooms: 3
Bathrooms: 2
Width: 52' - 10"
Depth: 50' - 6"
Foundation: Crawlspace, Slab

ORDER ONLINE @ EPLANS.COM

Everything needed for a family of four or a retired couple can be found in this charming country home. A 10-foot ceiling spans the gathering areas, which are anchored by a large fireplace and an angled breakfast bar. Two bedrooms and a bath open off a private hallway, and the master suite is secluded in the opposite corner of the plan. A spacious utility room and a storage area off the garage help keep clutter to a minimum.

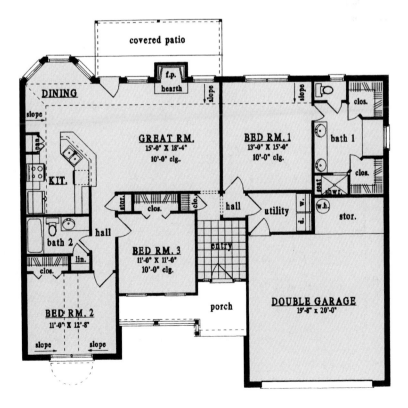

Perfectly symmetrical on the outside, this appealing home has an equally classic floor plan on the inside. A covered porch featuring full multipane windows opens directly to the spacious great room, which is open to the dining room and U-shaped kitchen for convenience and gracious entertaining. The kitchen connects to a roomy utility room with loads of counter space and windows overlooking the rear yard. The master suite lies to the front of the plan and has a view of the covered porch and a luxurious bath. Two family bedrooms reside to the rear of the plan; each has a window with backyard views.

plan # HPK1900019

Square Footage: 1,512
Bonus Space: 555 sq. ft.
Bedrooms: 3
Bathrooms: 2
Width: 60' - 0"
Depth: 38' - 0"
Foundation: Crawlspace, Unfinished Basement

ORDER ONLINE @ EPLANS.COM

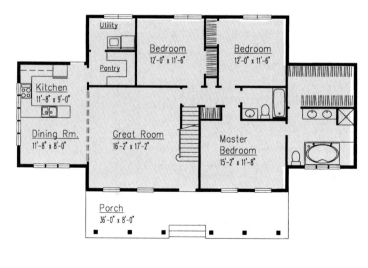

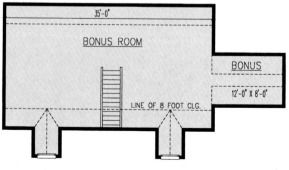

plan# HPK1900020

Square Footage: 2,225
Bonus Space: 302 sq. ft.
Bedrooms: 4
Bathrooms: 2
Width: 60' - 10"
Depth: 63' - 0"
Foundation: Crawlspace, Slab

ORDER ONLINE @ EPLANS.COM

A traditional country exterior hides a thoroughly modern open floor plan within. Nothing but a single column marking the corner of the dining room and an angled breakfast bar interrupt the flow of traffic and sightlines throughout the public areas of this home. Bedrooms are secluded in either wing; to the left, the master suite features a tall sloped ceiling and luxury bath. The right wing houses two secondary bedrooms and a high-ceilinged study, whose large closet and proximity to the hall bath could accommodate a fourth bedroom. Bonus space above the garage may be finished now or later, as needed.

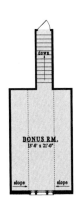

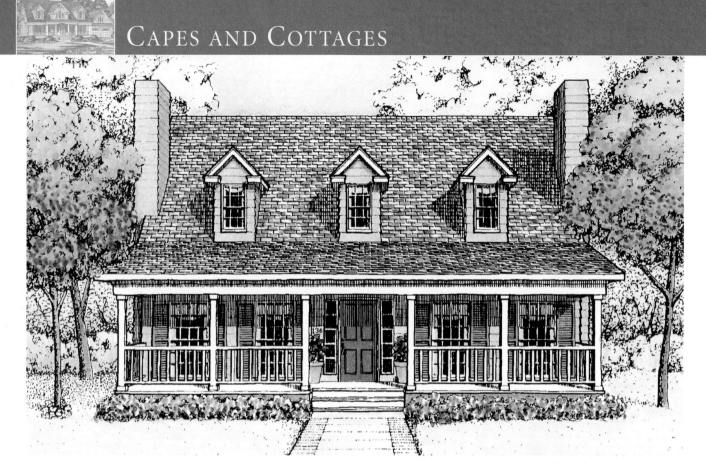

Simplicity is often the best approach to design. Twin chimneys serve as anchors to the home, and a deep front porch welcomes visitors. Inside, the cathedral ceiling and natural light from the dormers above enliven the great room. The well-appointed master suite also enjoys a private fireplace. Two additional bedrooms are located on the second floor along with the bonus room, which will add 115 square feet, if finished.

ptan# HPK1900021

First Floor: 1,152 sq. ft.
Second Floor: 567 sq. ft.
Total: 1,719 sq. ft.
Bonus Space: 115 sq. ft.
Bedrooms: 3
Bathrooms: 2½
Width: 36' - 0"
Depth: 64' - 0"
Foundation: Crawlspace,
Unfinished Basement

ORDER ONLINE @ EPLANS.COM

FIRST FLOOR

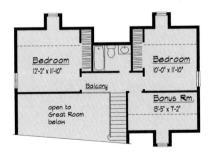

SECOND FLOOR

plan# HPK1900022

First Floor: 1,178 sq. ft.
Second Floor: 571 sq. ft.
Total: 1,749 sq. ft.
Bedrooms: 3
Bathrooms: 2½
Width: 38' - 0"
Depth: 45' - 0"
Foundation: Crawlspace,
Unfinished Basement

ORDER ONLINE @ EPLANS.COM

Symmetry pervades this fine three-bedroom home, from the three dormers and two chimneys to the attractive covered front porch. Inside, a living room offers a warming fireplace and has easy access to the L-shaped kitchen. Located on the first floor for privacy, the master suite is sure to please with a fireplace, large walk-in closet, second seasonal closet, dual-bowl vanity, and a separate tub and shower. Two secondary bedrooms reside upstairs and share a full bath and a balcony overlook to the foyer.

SECOND FLOOR

FIRST FLOOR

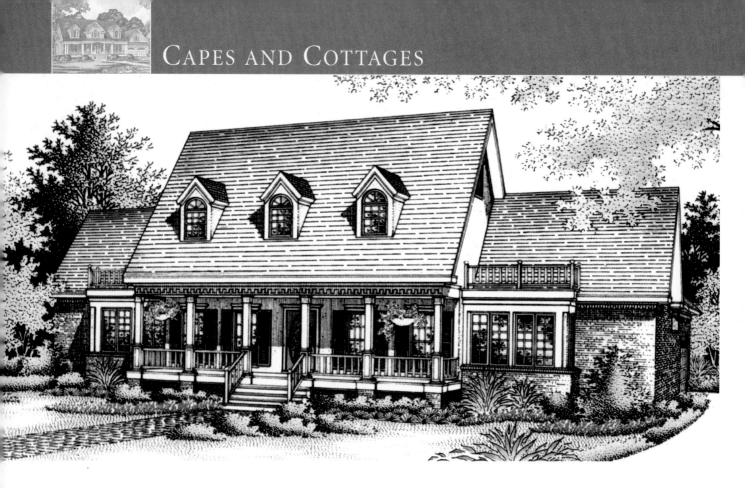

Dormer windows and a covered front porch lend a Southern country flavor to the exterior of this fine home. The interior is well planned and spacious. The living areas are open to one another and comprise a formal dining room, a family room with a sloped ceiling and fireplace, and a kitchen with an eating area. A huge pantry offers convenience to the kitchen. The master suite features a sitting area and large garden bath. The second floor holds two family bedrooms and a full bath. The balcony overlooks the family room below.

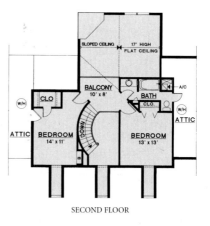

plan# HPK1900023

First Floor: 1,765 sq. ft.
Second Floor: 595 sq. ft.
Total: 2,360 sq. ft.
Bedrooms: 3
Bathrooms: 2½
Width: 68' - 0"
Depth: 74' - 0"
Foundation: Unfinished Basement, Slab, Crawlspace

ORDER ONLINE @ EPLANS.COM

FIRST FLOOR

SECOND FLOOR

© WILLIAM E POOLE DESIGNS, INC.

plan# HPK1900024

First Floor: 1,832 sq. ft.

Second Floor: 574 sq. ft.

Total: 2,406 sq. ft.

Bonus Space: 410 sq. ft.

Bedrooms: 4

Bathrooms: 3

Width: 77' - 10"

Depth: 41' - 4"

Foundation: Crawlspace

ORDER ONLINE @ EPLANS.COM

This farmhouse style welcomes you with shuttered windows and doorway, and covered front and side porches. An open floor plan with an inside balcony creates a feeling of expansiveness. French doors; a gathering room with fireplace and access to the terrace; a kitchen with pantry, island, and breakfast nook; and everything the inhabitants of the master and one family bedroom will ever need round out the main floor. Upstairs, find bedrooms 3 and 4, a media center, and a great view to below.

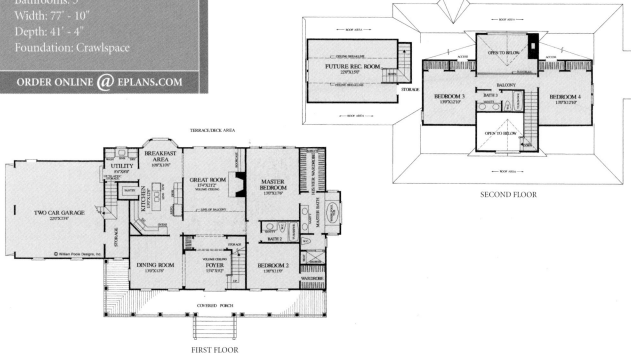

FIRST FLOOR

SECOND FLOOR

© William E. Poole Designs, Inc.

Three petite dormers top a welcoming covered porch and add a touch of grace to an already beautiful home. Inside, the foyer opens to the left to a formal dining room, which in turn has easy access to the efficient kitchen. Here, a pantry and a snack bar in the breakfast area make meal preparations a delight. The nearby spacious family room features a fireplace, built-in bookshelves, and outdoor access. Located away from the master suite for privacy, two family bedrooms pamper with private baths and walk-in closets. On the other end of the home, the master suite provides luxury via a huge walk-in closet, whirlpool tub, and corner shower with a seat. An optional second floor features a fourth bedroom in private splendor with its own bath and access to a recreation room complete with a second fireplace.

plan# HPK1900025

Square Footage: 2,215
Bonus Space: 636 sq. ft.
Bedrooms: 3
Bathrooms: 3
Width: 69' - 10"
Depth: 62' - 6"
Foundation: Crawlspace, Unfinished Basement

ORDER ONLINE @ EPLANS.COM

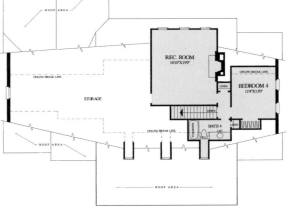

© William E. Poole Designs, Inc.

plan# HPK1900026

First Floor: 1,556 sq. ft.
Second Floor: 623 sq. ft.
Total: 2,179 sq. ft.
Bonus Space: 368 sq. ft.
Bedrooms: 3
Bathrooms: 2½
Width: 73' - 4"
Depth: 41' - 4"
Foundation: Crawlspace, Finished Basement

ORDER ONLINE @ EPLANS.COM

This charming farmhouse starts out with a welcoming front porch lined with columns. Inside, the foyer opens to the right to the formal dining room. At the rear of the home, a two-story great room provides a fireplace, built-ins, and direct access to the backyard. The nearby kitchen is complete with a walk-in pantry and an adjacent breakfast area. The first-floor master suite offers a large walk-in closet and a pampering bath. Upstairs, two family bedrooms share a hall bath.

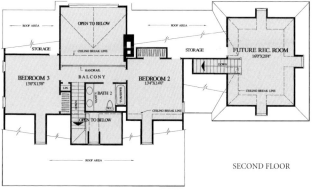

SECOND FLOOR

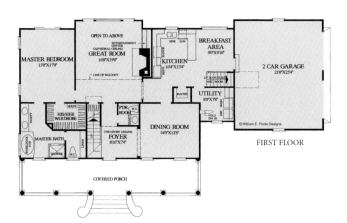

FIRST FLOOR

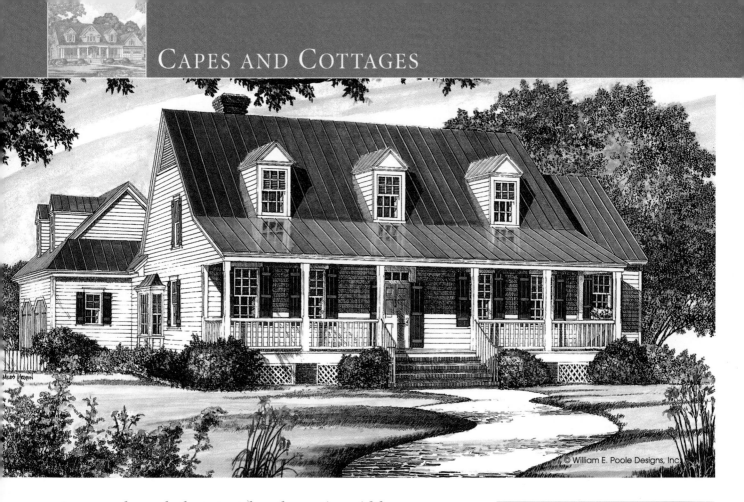

© William E. Poole Designs, Inc

A covered porch that stretches the entire width of the house welcomes friends and family to this fine four-bedroom home. Inside, the foyer is flanked by the staircase to the right and an arched opening into the formal dining room to the left. The great room, with a two-story ceiling, fireplace, and wall of windows, has easy access to the bayed breakfast area and the efficient kitchen. Two bedrooms occupy this level—one a lavish master suite complete with a walk-in closet and pampering bath, the other a family bedroom with easy access to a full bath. Upstairs, two more bedrooms share a hall bath and a balcony overlooking the great room.

plan # HPK1900027

First Floor: 1,776 sq. ft.
Second Floor: 643 sq. ft.
Total: 2,419 sq. ft.
Bonus Space: 367 sq. ft.
Bedrooms: 4
Bathrooms: 3
Width: 61' - 8"
Depth: 74' - 4"
Foundation: Unfinished Basement, Crawlspace

ORDER ONLINE @ EPLANS.COM

FIRST FLOOR

SECOND FLOOR

© WILLIAM E POOLE DESIGNS, INC.

plan# HPK1900028

Square Footage: 2,777
Bonus Space: 424 sq. ft.
Bedrooms: 3
Bathrooms: 2½
Width: 75' - 6"
Depth: 60' - 2"
Foundation: Crawlspace, Unfinished Basement

ORDER ONLINE @ EPLANS.COM

This home is an absolute dream when it comes to living space! Whether formal or casual, there's a room for every occasion. The foyer opens to the formal dining room on the left; straight ahead lies the magnificent hearth-warmed living room. The island kitchen opens not only to a breakfast nook, but to a huge family/sunroom surrounded by two walls of windows! The right wing of the plan holds the sleeping quarters—two family bedrooms sharing a bath, and a majestic master suite. The second floor holds an abundance of expandable space.

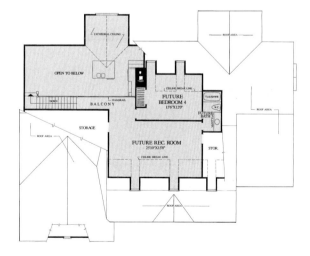

This home plan is so comprehensive, you won't believe that there is bonus space included. A covered porch accesses a foyer with adjoining open formal dining area leading to the stunning great room, past decorative columns. The master suite is partitioned to the right of the great room, and features a stylish tray ceiling and luscious vaulted bath behind a French door. A separate bedroom is hidden away with its own bath. An ultra-functional kitchen lies to the left of the great room, with an open space adjoining the breakfast area to the latter. The nook opens to the patio via a French door, and affords a panoramic outdoor view through a bayed window. Around a built-in desk and walk-in pantry are the laundry and two bedrooms with shared bath. The staircase and interior access to the garage are located back through the kitchen.

plan ⊕ # HPK1900029

Square Footage: 2,050
Bonus Space: 418 sq. ft.
Bedrooms: 4
Bathrooms: 3
Width: 60' - 0"
Depth: 56' - 0"
Foundation: Crawlspace, Unfinished
Walkout Basement, Slab

ORDER ONLINE @ EPLANS.COM

plan # HPK1900030

Square Footage: 1,749
Bonus Space: 327 sq. ft.
Bedrooms: 3
Bathrooms: 2
Width: 54' - 0"
Depth: 56' - 6"
Foundation: Unfinished Walkout
Basement, Slab, Crawlspace

ORDER ONLINE @ EPLANS.COM

This cozy country cottage is enhanced with a front-facing planter box above the garage and a charming covered porch. The foyer leads to a vaulted great room, complete with a fireplace and radius windows. Decorative columns complement the entrance to the dining room, as does the arched opening. On the left side of the plan resides the master suite, which is resplendent with amenities including a vaulted sitting room with an arched entryway, tray ceiling, and French doors to the vaulted full bath. On the right side, two additional bedrooms share a full bath.

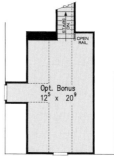

OPTIONAL BONUS ROOM PLAN

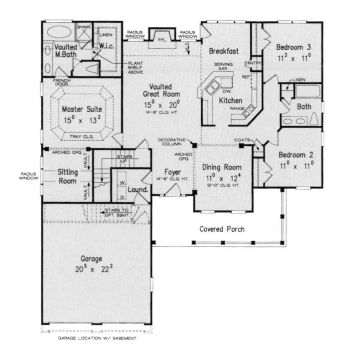

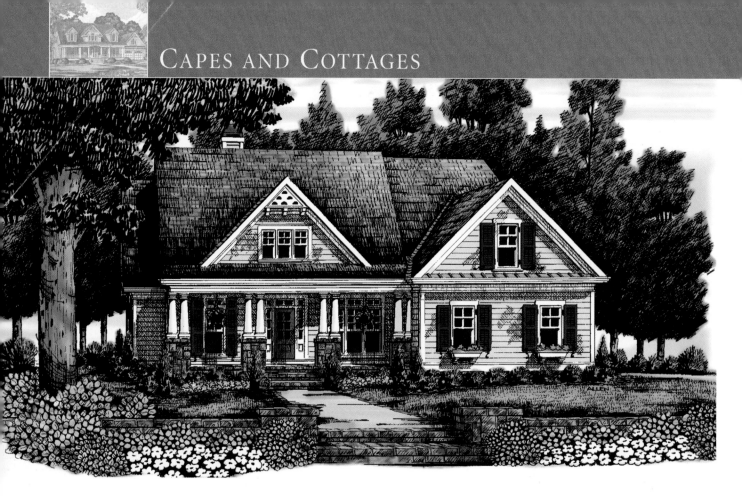

Cheerful window shutters and a covered front porch welcome you home at day's end. A two-story foyer sets the tone for indulgence inside, with the formal dining room opening off immediately to the right. A vaulted family room awaits at the other end, affording ambient sunlight through a radius transom. The adjacent kitchen connects to a screened porch through the breakfast area and a French door. A family bedroom is on the other side of the kitchen, with the laundry, a full bath, closets, and garage access nearby. The left wing of the plan is reserved for the palatial master suite, with beamed ceilings in the bedroom, and a vaulted bath. Upstairs are two family bedrooms with respective walk-in closets, attic space, and a bonus room.

plan# HPK1900031

First Floor: 1,774 sq. ft.
Second Floor: 525 sq. ft.
Total: 2,299 sq. ft.
Bonus Space: 300 sq. ft.
Bedrooms: 4
Bathrooms: 3
Width: 56' - 0"
Depth: 63' - 4"
Foundation: Crawlspace, Unfinished Walkout Basement, Slab

ORDER ONLINE @ EPLANS.COM

FIRST FLOOR

SECOND FLOOR

© 2004 by Designer, All Rights Reserved

plan# HPK1900032

First Floor: 1,755 sq. ft.

Second Floor: 864 sq. ft.

Total: 2,619 sq. ft.

Bedrooms: 4

Bathrooms: 3½

Width: 56' - 0"

Depth: 53' - 0"

Foundation: Crawlspace, Unfinished Walkout Basement, Slab

ORDER ONLINE @ EPLANS.COM

Open-face gables, broad white trim, and double-hung window sashes create appeal on this cottage's exterior. Inside, a comfortable and modern design of the great room caters to the active family requiring more functional than formal space. The island kitchen will be a favorite hangout. A formal dining room is perfect for entertaining and hosting holiday meals. A first-floor master suite includes an amenity-filled bath and imperial-sized walk-in closet. Upstairs, three secondary bedrooms share two full baths.

SECOND FLOOR

FIRST FLOOR

© 2004 by Designer, All Rights Reserved

Come home to this delightful bungalow, created with you in mind. From the covered front porch, the foyer opens to the dining room on the left and vaulted family room ahead. An elongated island in the well-planned kitchen makes meal preparation a joy. A sunny breakfast nook is perfect for casual pursuits. Tucked to the rear, the master suite enjoys ultimate privacy and a luxurious break from the world with a vaulted bath and garden tub. Secondary bedrooms share a full bath upstairs; a bonus room is ready to expand as your needs change.

plan # HPK1900033

First Floor: 1,561 sq. ft.
Second Floor: 578 sq. ft.
Total: 2,139 sq. ft.
Bonus Space: 238 sq. ft.
Bedrooms: 3
Bathrooms: 2½
Width: 50' - 0"
Depth: 56' - 6"
Foundation: Crawlspace, Unfinished
Walkout Basement, Slab

ORDER ONLINE @ EPLANS.COM

FIRST FLOOR

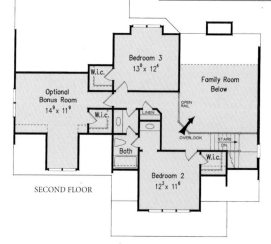

SECOND FLOOR

plan# HPK1900034

First Floor: 1,060 sq. ft.
Second Floor: 914 sq. ft.
Total: 1,974 sq. ft.
Bedrooms: 3
Bathrooms: 3
Width: 32' - 0"
Depth: 35' - 0"
Foundation: Crawlspace

ORDER ONLINE @ EPLANS.COM

This charming Craftsman design offers a second-story master bedroom with four windows under the gabled dormer. The covered front porch displays column and pier supports. The hearth-warmed gathering room opens to the dining room on the right, where the adjoining kitchen offers enough space for an optional breakfast booth. A home office/guest suite is found in the rear. The second floor holds the lavish master suite and a second bedroom suite with its own private bath.

FIRST FLOOR

SECOND FLOOR

Looking for a flexible home?

This is it: a comfortable one-level Cape Cod with future space built in to the design. The bonus second floor is dedicated to fitting your family as needed. The complete first floor boasts two family bedrooms sharing a full bath, an open kitchen with an adjoining dining bay, and a capacious great room with rear-porch access and a warm fireplace. The master suite enjoys privacy and a full bath.

plan# HPK1900035

Square Footage: 1,644
Bonus Space: 922 sq. ft.
Bedrooms: 3
Bathrooms: 2
Width: 63' - 0"
Depth: 52' - 2"
Foundation: Crawlspace, Slab, Unfinished Basement

ORDER ONLINE @ EPLANS.COM

OPTIONAL LAYOUT

Laundry
To Optional Basement
To Optional Upstairs
Garage
Porch

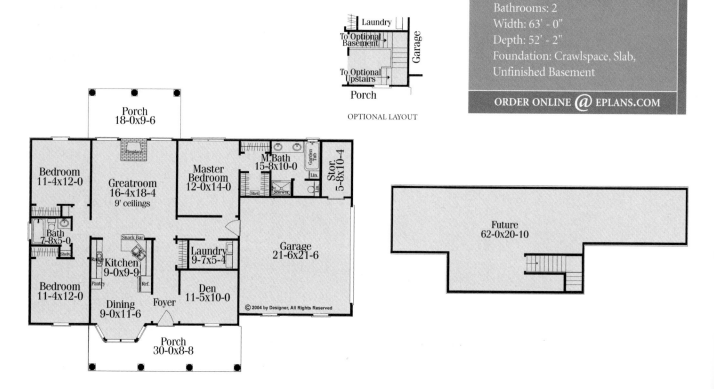

Porch 18-0x9-6

Bedroom 11-4x12-0

Greatroom 16-4x18-4
9' ceilings

Master Bedroom 12-0x14-0

M. Bath 15-8x10-0

Stor. 5-8x10-4

Garden Tub

Bath 7-8x5-0

Snack Bar

Kitchen 9-0x9-9

Laundry 9-7x5-4

Garage 21-6x21-6

Bedroom 11-4x12-0

Pantry

Dining 9-0x11-6

Foyer

Den 11-5x10-0

Porch 30-0x8-8

© 2004 by Designer, All Rights Reserved

Future 62-0x20-10

plan# HPK1900036

First Floor: 1,440 sq. ft.

Second Floor: 1,514 sq. ft.

Total: 2,954 sq. ft.

Bonus Space: 719 sq. ft.

Bedrooms: 4

Bathrooms: 3½

Width: 30' - 0"

Depth: 68' - 0"

Foundation: Unfinished Walkout Basement

ORDER ONLINE @ EPLANS.COM

A stylish Craftsman at just under 3,000 square feet, this home features an open layout ideal for entertaining. Rooms are distinguished by columns, eliminating the use of unnecessary walls. At the rear of the home, the expansive family room, warmed by a fireplace, faces the adjoining breakfast area and kitchen. Access to the sundeck makes alfresco meals an option. A walk-in pantry is an added bonus. The second floor houses the family bedrooms, including the lavish master suite, two bedrooms separated by a Jack-and-Jill bath, and a fourth bedroom with a private, full bath. The second-floor laundry room is smart and convenient. A centrally located, optional computer station is perfect for a family computer. A sizable recreation room on the basement level completes this plan.

OPTIONAL LAYOUT

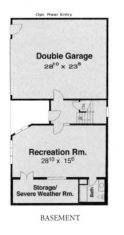

BASEMENT

FIRST FLOOR

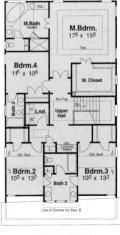

SECOND FLOOR

Columns, transoms, and a clerestory lend this house a stylish country charm. Inside, a built-in media center, a fireplace, and columns add to the wonderful livability of this home. The modified galley kitchen features a serving bar and an island workstation. Escape to the relaxing master suite featuring a private sitting room and a luxurious bath set between His and Hers walk-in closets. Three bedrooms share a bath on the other side of the plan, ensuring privacy. Note the handy storage area in the two-car, side-entry garage.

plan# HPK1900037

Square Footage: 2,360
Bedrooms: 4
Bathrooms: 2
Width: 75' - 2"
Depth: 68' - 0"
Foundation: Crawlspace, Slab, Unfinished Basement

ORDER ONLINE @ EPLANS.COM

Basement Stair Location

plan# HPK1900038

First Floor: 1,294 sq. ft.

Second Floor: 1,220 sq. ft.

Total: 2,514 sq. ft.

Bonus Space: 366 sq. ft.

Bedrooms: 3

Bathrooms: 2½

Width: 38' - 0"

Depth: 76' - 0"

Foundation: Unfinished Walkout Basement

ORDER ONLINE @ EPLANS.COM

The unassuming facade of this traditional home offers few clues about how ideal this deisgn is for entertaining. The lack of unnecessary walls achieves a clean, smart layout that flows seamlessly. A side deck accessed from the living room and breakfast area extends the gathering outside. Upstairs houses all of the family bedrooms, including the master suite, enhanced by a spacious private deck. Two additional family bedrooms share a full bath. A bonus fourth bedroom boasts a full bath and could be used as a recreation/exercise/guest room. The central study/loft area is perfect for a family computer.

OPTIONAL LAYOUT

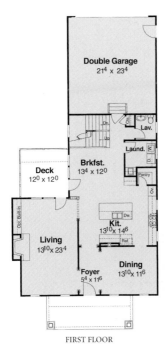

FIRST FLOOR

SECOND FLOOR

Compact and perfect for starters or empty-nesters, this is a wonderful single-level home. The beautiful facade is supplemented by a stylish and practical covered porch. Just to the left of the entry is a roomy kitchen with bright windows and convenient storage. The octagonal dining room shares a three-sided fireplace with the living room. A covered patio to the rear enhances outdoor living. A fine master suite enjoys a grand bath and is complemented by a secondary bedroom and full bath.

plan# HPK1900039

Square Footage: 1,118
Bedrooms: 2
Bathrooms: 2
Width: 44' - 4"
Depth: 47' - 4"
Foundation: Slab

ORDER ONLINE @ EPLANS.COM

© 1998 Donald A. Gardner, Inc.

B. NATHAN

plan # HPK1900040

Square Footage: 1,476
Bonus Space: 340 sq. ft.
Bedrooms: 3
Bathrooms: 2
Width: 63' - 4"
Depth: 46' - 10"

ORDER ONLINE @ EPLANS.COM

This country plan begins with crisp horizontal wood siding and an arched entry with sidelights. The foyer opens to a great room with a fireplace and cathedral ceiling. A door in the great room leads out to a covered porch with skylights. Columns and a tray ceiling define the dining room and the peninsula kitchen sits nearby. The master suite features a tray ceiling, plus a bath with a walk-in closet, double sinks, and separate tub and shower. Note the bonus room over the garage, which is reached via a staircase behind the utility room.

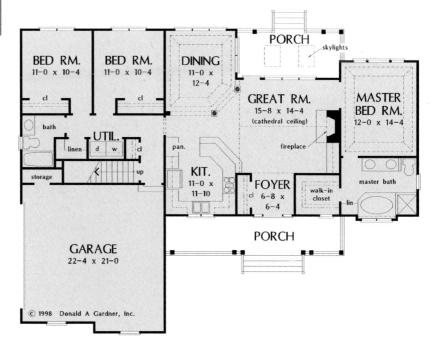

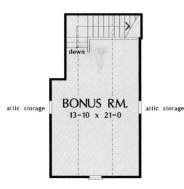

©1998 Donald A. Gardner, Inc.

Stunning arched windows framed by bold front-facing gables add to the tremendous curb appeal of this modest home. Topped by a cathedral ceiling and with porches on either side, the great room is expanded further by its openness to the dining room and kitchen. Flexibility, which is so important in a home this size, is found in the versatile bedroom/study as well as the bonus room over the garage. The master suite is positioned for privacy at the rear of the home, with a graceful tray ceiling, walk-in closet, and private bath. An additional bedroom and a hall bath complete the plan.

plan# HPK1900041

Square Footage: 1,428
Bonus Space: 313 sq. ft.
Bedrooms: 3
Bathrooms: 2
Width: 52' - 8"
Depth: 52' - 4"

ORDER ONLINE @ EPLANS.COM

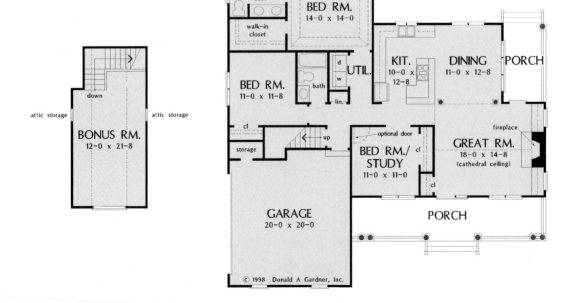

© 1999 Donald A. Gardner, Inc.

plan# HPK1900042

Square Footage: 1,882
Bonus Space: 363 sq. ft.
Bedrooms: 3
Bathrooms: 2½
Width: 61' - 4"
Depth: 55' - 0"

ORDER ONLINE @ EPLANS.COM

An arched window in a center front-facing gable lends style and beauty to the facade of this three-bedroom home. An open common area features a great room with a cathedral ceiling, a formal dining room with a tray ceiling, a functional kitchen, and an informal breakfast area that separates the master suite from the secondary bedrooms for privacy. The master suite provides a dramatic vaulted ceiling, access to the back porch, and abundant closet space. Access to a versatile bonus room is near the master bedroom.

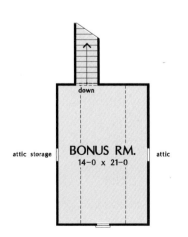

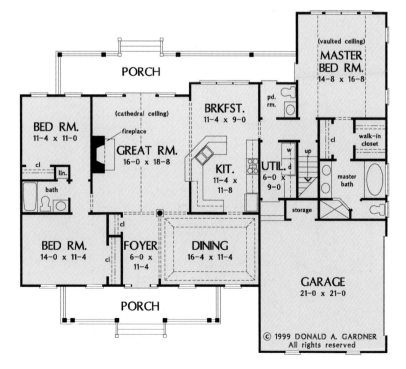

© 1999 DONALD A. GARDNER
All rights reserved

© 1997 Donald A. Gardner Architects, Inc.

With an exciting blend of styles, this home combines the wrapping porch of a country farmhouse with a brick-and-siding exterior for a uniquely pleasing effect. The great room shares its cathedral ceiling with an open kitchen, and the octagonal dining room is complemented by a tray ceiling. Built-ins flank the great room's fireplace for added convenience. The master suite features a full bath, a walk-in closet, and access to the rear porch. Two additional bedrooms share a full hall bath; a third can be converted into a study. Skylit bonus space is available above the garage, which is connected to the home by a covered breezeway.

plan # HPK1900043

Square Footage: 2,273
Bonus Space: 342 sq. ft.
Bedrooms: 4
Bathrooms: 2½
Width: 74' - 8"
Depth: 75' - 10"

ORDER ONLINE @ EPLANS.COM

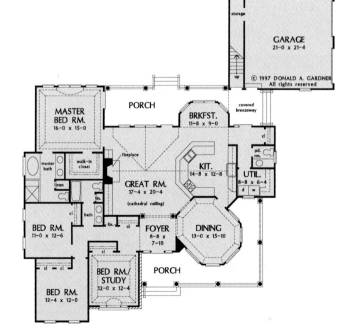

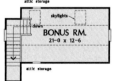

© 1999 Donald A. Gardner, Inc.

plan# HPK1900044

Square Footage: 2,078
Bonus Space: 339 sq. ft.
Bedrooms: 3
Bathrooms: 2½
Width: 62' - 2"
Depth: 47' - 8"

ORDER ONLINE @ EPLANS.COM

An enchanting L-shaped front porch lends charm and grace to this country home with dual dormers and gables. Bay windows expand both of the home's dining areas; the great room and kitchen are amplified by a shared cathedral ceiling. The generous great room features a fireplace with flanking built-ins, skylights, and access to a marvelous back porch. A cathedral ceiling enhances the master suite, which enjoys a large walk-in closet and a luxurious bath. Two more bedrooms share a generous hall bath that has a dual-sink vanity.

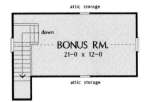

©1999 Donald A. Gardner, Inc.

Colonial style meets farmhouse charm in this plan, furnishing old-fashioned charisma with a flourish. From the entry, double doors open to the country dining room and a large island kitchen. Nearby, the spacious great room takes center stage and is warmed by a fireplace flanked by large windows. Tucked behind the three-car garage, the secluded master suite features a vaulted ceiling. The master bath contains a relaxing tub, double-bowl vanity, separate shower, and compartmented toilet. Beyond the bath is a huge walk-in closet with two built-in chests. Three family bedrooms—one doubles as a study or home office—a full bath, and a utility room complete the plan.

plan# HPK1900045

Square Footage: 2,078
Bedrooms: 4
Bathrooms: 2
Width: 75' - 0"
Depth: 47' - 10"
Foundation: Slab, Crawlspace

ORDER ONLINE @ EPLANS.COM

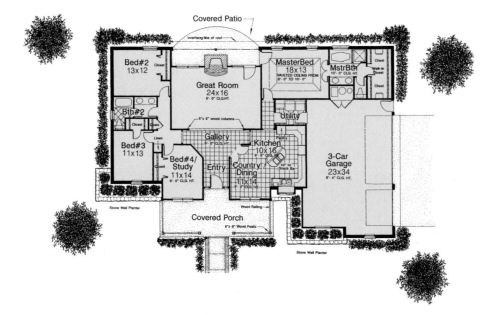

plan# HPK1900046

Square Footage: 1,380
Bonus Space: 372 sq. ft.
Bedrooms: 3
Bathrooms: 2
Width: 48' - 0"
Depth: 43' - 4"
Foundation: Crawlspace, Slab, Unfinished Basement

ORDER ONLINE @ EPLANS.COM

Here is a starter home that is quaint and cozy yet spacious, including three bedrooms, and bonus space on the second floor for future expansion. The double-door entry opens to the great room where a wall of windows looks out to the rear deck. The dining room with a sunny bay window sits beyond a dramatic arch to the right. The U-shaped kitchen adjoins the dining room with the utility and laundry rooms close at hand. The master suite offers privacy on the right, and two family bedrooms share a full bath on the left.

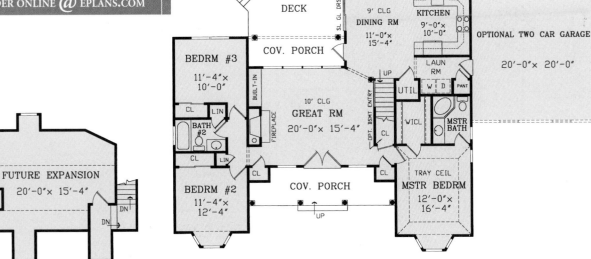

A covered porch opens the way to interior spaces—a main level with living spaces and the master suite, and an upper level with two family bedrooms. Designed for the way you live, the great room is vaulted and open to a dining area and handy kitchen. A fireplace warms the gathering area. Corner built-ins in the dining room frame a window and door to the vaulted back porch. The front office also has space for optional built-ins. A side hallway leads back to the master suite. Upper level bedrooms enjoy the use of a full bath that separates them. A shop area in the garage is an added bonus.

plan# HPK1900047

First Floor: 1,603 sq. ft.
Second Floor: 471 sq. ft.
Total: 2,074 sq. ft.
Bedrooms: 3
Bathrooms: 2½
Width: 50' - 0"
Depth: 56' - 0"
Foundation: Crawlspace

ORDER ONLINE @ EPLANS.COM

FIRST FLOOR

SECOND FLOOR

ORDER BLUEPRINTS 24 HOURS, 7 DAYS A WEEK, AT 1-800-521-6797

plan# HPK1900048

Square Footage: 1,484 sq. ft.
Bonus Space: 484 sq. ft.
Bedrooms: 3
Bathrooms: 2
Width: 38' - 0"
Depth: 70' - 0"
Foundation: Crawlspace

ORDER ONLINE @ EPLANS.COM

Ideal for narrow lots, this fine bungalow is full of amenities. The entry is just off a covered front porch and leads to a living room complete with a fireplace. The formal dining room is nearby and works well with the L-shaped kitchen. The breakfast nook opens onto a rear patio. Sleeping quarters consist of a master suite with a walk-in closet and private bath, as well as two family bedrooms sharing a full bath. An unfinished attic awaits future development; a two-car garage easily shelters the family vehicles.

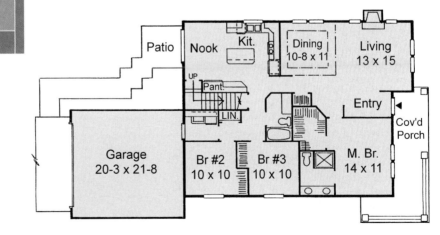

Patio
Nook
Kit.
Dining 10-8 x 11
Living 13 x 15
UP
Pant
LIN.
Entry
Cov'd Porch
Garage 20-3 x 21-8
Br #2 10 x 10
Br #3 10 x 10
M. Br. 14 x 11

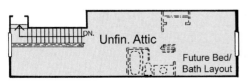

DN.
Unfin. Attic
Future Bed/ Bath Layout

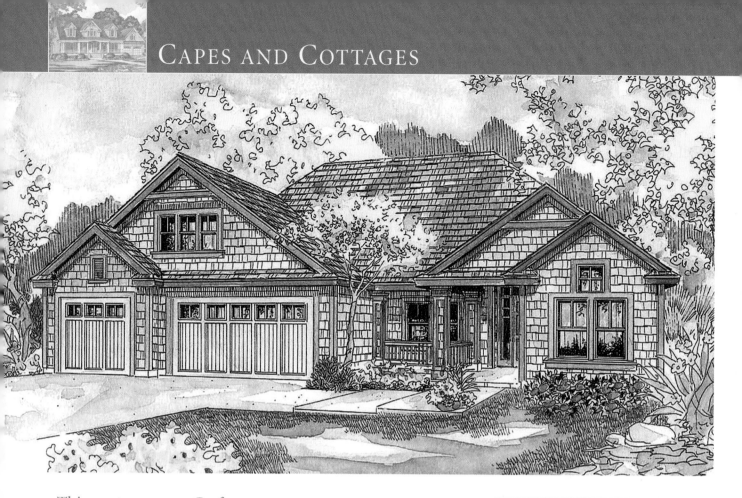

This contemporary Craftsman-style bungalow fits right in beside an ocean or lake, and is equally adaptable for year-round living in a suburban neighborhood. Plenty of natural light beams into the vaulted foyer through sidelights and a wide transom. Double doors on the left access a vaulted room that could be a den or home office. The foyer opens to the spacious, vaulted living room, where windows fill most of the rear wall. A gas fireplace nestles into the far corner at the window's edge. Opposite the fireplace, two openings lead to the kitchen and dinette. A long, raised eating bar is great for snacking, chatting, and homework supervision. In the kitchen there's plenty of counter and cupboard space, built-in appliances, and a walk-in pantry. Laundry appliances are located in a utility room that connects to the three-car garage. In the far corner of the home, the master suite features a luxury bath and patio access. Two secondary bedrooms and a bath open from a small hallway off the foyer.

plan# HPK1900049

Square Footage: 2,103
Bonus Space: 414 sq. ft.
Bedrooms: 3
Bathrooms: 2
Width: 66' - 0"
Depth: 64' - 0"
Foundation: Crawlspace

ORDER ONLINE @ EPLANS.COM

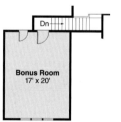

Bonus Room
17' x 20'

Dn

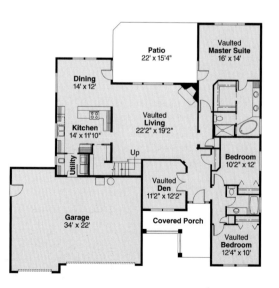

Patio
22' x 15'4"

Vaulted
Master Suite
16' x 14'

Dining
14' x 12'

Vaulted
Living
22'2" x 19'2"

Kitchen
14' x 11'10"

Utility

Up

Bedroom
10'2" x 12'

Vaulted
Den
11'2" x 12'2"

Garage
34' x 22'

Covered Porch

Vaulted
Bedroom
12'4" x 10'

plan# HPK1900050

Square Footage: 2,009
Bonus Space: 489 sq. ft.
Bedrooms: 3
Bathrooms: 2
Width: 60' - 0"
Depth: 54' - 0"
Foundation: Crawlspace

ORDER ONLINE @ EPLANS.COM

If this plan doesn't remind you of your childhood home, perhaps it looks like one you wish you'd grown up in. Its appearance is at once solid, warm, and comfortably unpretentious. Two wide banks of gridded windows sparkle across the recessed front porch, creating a sense of openness. Inside, the living room and dining room are located to the left and right of the foyer, and a spacious family room lies directly ahead. A gas fireplace nestles into one rear corner, at the end of a long wall of windows. In the opposite corner, a raised eating bar offers a natural area for family and friends to settle in for a chat with the chef. The master suite boasts a deep soaking tub, plus a separately enclosed shower and toilet. Secondary bedrooms and a bathroom are on the other side of the plan. Upstairs, bonus space offers possibility and flexibility.

This Craftsman-flavored Cape Cod is thoroughly modern on the inside. Vaulted ceilings span the open floor plan, anchored by a spacious great room with corner fireplace. Family activities will gravitate towards this space and its satellites: an airy breakfast nook and storage-rich kitchen. Pocket doors separate the kitchen from the formal dining room, where walls of windows bring in natural light. The master suite boasts a deep soaking tub, over-sized cultured marble shower, and twin vanities. Two upstairs bedrooms share a compartmented bath, and a huge bonus room may be finished off as a fourth bedroom, rec room, or exercise room.

plan ⊕ HPK1900051

First Floor: 1,875 sq. ft.
Second Floor: 622 sq. ft.
Total: 2,497 sq. ft.
Bonus Space: 374 sq. ft.
Bedrooms: 3
Bathrooms: 2½
Width: 53' - 0"
Depth: 66' - 0"
Foundation: Crawlspace

ORDER ONLINE @ EPLANS.COM

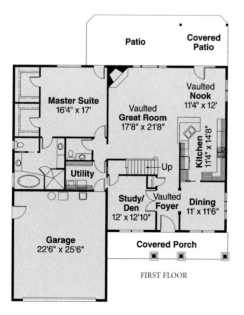

FIRST FLOOR

SECOND FLOOR

plan⊕ HPK1900052

First Floor: 1,599 sq. ft.
Second Floor: 611 sq. ft.
Total: 2,210 sq. ft.
Bonus Space: 230 sq. ft.
Bedrooms: 3
Bathrooms: 2½
Width: 55' - 0"
Depth: 52' - 0"
Foundation: Crawlspace

ORDER ONLINE @ EPLANS.COM

This Craftsman-style cottage offers fine vistas from all rear rooms on the main floor. In the great room, a gas fireplace flanked by wide, tall windows creates a focal point. This lofty space is totally open to the nook and kitchen. Glass doors in the nook slide open to let in summer breezes and provide easy access to a partially covered patio. Counters and cupboards wrap around three sides of the spacious kitchen. A central island creates additional storage and work space, and a walk-in pantry fills one entire corner. The built-in desk is perfect for keeping on top of household bills. Laundry appliances and a powder room are close by. The master suite, which fills the left wing, boasts a huge walk-in closet and roomy bathroom. Two more bedrooms share a split bath upstairs.

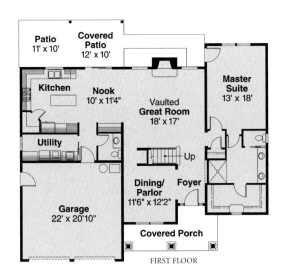

FIRST FLOOR

SECOND FLOOR

A cedar-shake exterior gives this home a handcrafted look that blends right in with a natural environment. Built high on a mountain slope, or overlooking a lake, river, or ocean, the home's hexagonal shape and walls of windows enable stunning views from almost every room. The wide deck that wraps around the back of the home allows family and friends to move outdoors for an even closer look, when the weather is inviting. A vaulted living area is at the core of the plan, while short wings containing the bedrooms extend from either side. Inviting gas fireplaces highlight the living room and master suite. Kitchen amenities include a long snack bar, a walk-in pantry, and a generous supply of cupboards and counter space. A spiral stairway at center circles up to a loft.

plan# HPK1900053

First Floor: 2,372 sq. ft.
Second Floor: 263 sq. ft.
Total: 2,635 sq. ft.
Bedrooms: 3
Bathrooms: 2
Width: 83' - 0"
Depth: 75' - 0"
Foundation: Unfinished Walkout Basement

ORDER ONLINE @ EPLANS.COM

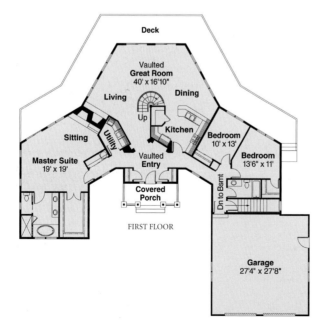

FIRST FLOOR

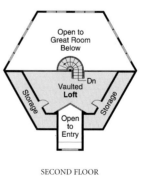

SECOND FLOOR

plan # HPK1900054

Square Footage: 1,822
Bedrooms: 3
Bathrooms: 2
Width: 58' - 0"
Depth: 67' - 2"
Foundation: Crawlspace

ORDER ONLINE @ EPLANS.COM

Stone bays and wood siding make up the exterior facade on this one-story home. The interior revolves around the living room with an attached dining room and the galley kitchen with a breakfast room. The master suite has a fine bath and a walk-in closet. One of three family bedrooms on the left side of the plan could be used as a home office.

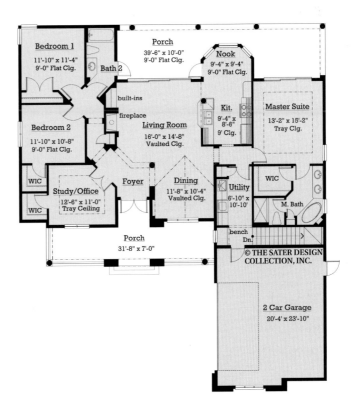

Craftsman styling warms this country home, with its extensive covered porch that turns the corner with lots of charm and an invitation for outdoor living at its best. In a departure from cottage architecture of the past, the main-floor living spaces in this contemporary rendering of the bungalow are open and airy. A master bedroom suite allows empty-nesters to live on a single level, or gives parents a separate retreat that is still within hailing distance of the rooms upstairs. A balcony on the second floor overlooks the main living spaces and connects the three bedrooms. A laundry room off the two-car garage and a home office off the kitchen promise efficient work space out of the main stream of activity.

plan # HPK1900055

First Floor: 1,711 sq. ft.
Second Floor: 805 sq. ft.
Total: 2,516 sq. ft.
Bonus Space: 288 sq. ft.
Bedrooms: 4
Bathrooms: 3½
Width: 50' - 8"
Depth: 62' - 0"
Foundation: Unfinished Basement

ORDER ONLINE @ EPLANS.COM

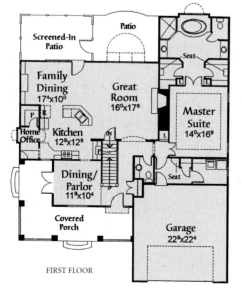

FIRST FLOOR

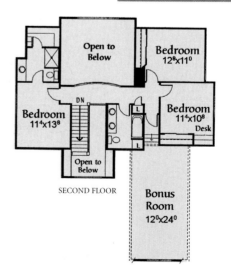

SECOND FLOOR

plan# HPK1900056

Total: 2,842 sq. ft.
Bonus Space: 1,172 sq. ft.
Bedrooms: 3
Bathrooms: 2½
Width: 91' - 0"
Depth: 69' - 4"
Foundation: Slab

ORDER ONLINE @ EPLANS.COM

This country-style home is lovely to behold and economical to build. Front and back covered porches create a warm transition to the yard, where a charming porte cochere gives shelter to those disembarking from vehicles. From the dining room, steps lead down to the sunken family room with a warming fireplace. A second set of steps leads up to the main hallway, which connects the living room with the master suite and two roomy bedrooms. The master bedroom features private access to the rear porch, two walk-in closets, and a well-appointed bathroom. Room to grow is available in the unfinished space on the second floor.

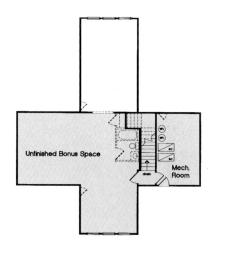

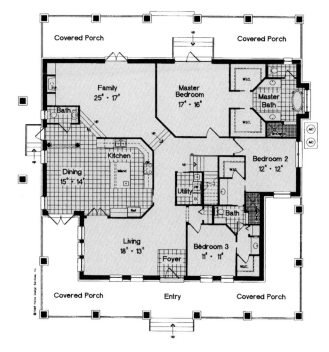

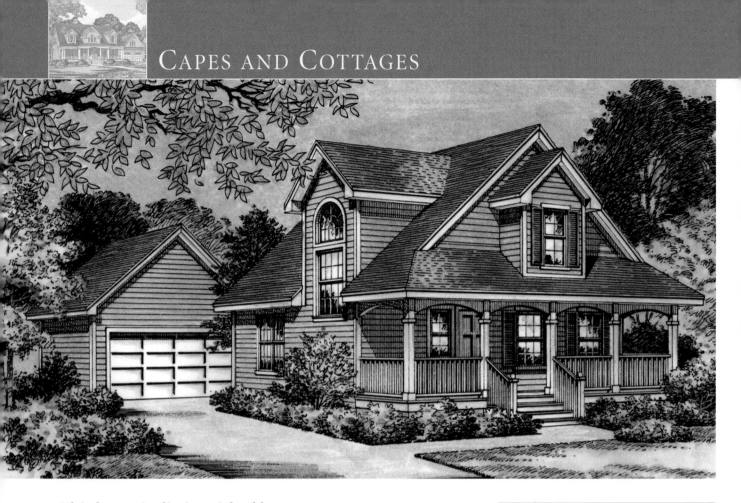

This home is distinguished by its two prominent dormers—one facing front and the other on the left side. The dormer to the left boasts a sunburst window that spills light into the family room. Enter through a large covered porch to a foyer that looks into the family room. Beyond, a vaulted kitchen/nook area is graced with an abundance of windows and rear-door access. The master bedroom is located at the front of the plan, and is accented with a full bath. On the second floor are two additional bedrooms, each with ample closet space.

plan# HPK1900057

First Floor: 820 sq. ft.
Second Floor: 350 sq. ft.
Total: 1,170 sq. ft.
Bedrooms: 3
Bathrooms: 2
Width: 37' - 0"
Depth: 67' - 0"
Foundation: Slab

ORDER ONLINE @ EPLANS.COM

FIRST FLOOR

SECOND FLOOR

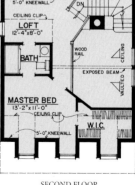

plan# HPK1900058

First Floor: 576 sq. ft.
Second Floor: 489 sq. ft.
Total: 1,065 sq. ft.
Bedrooms: 1
Bathrooms: 1½
Width: 24' - 0"
Depth: 31' - 0"
Foundation: Crawlspace

ORDER ONLINE @ EPLANS.COM

The steep rooflines on this home offer a sophisticated look that draws attention. Three dormers flood the home with light. Detailed porch supports lend a Gothic feel to the entry, which leads to the two-story living room complete with a fireplace. The dining room is quite spacious and contains convenient access to the kitchen where a pantry room and plenty of counter space make cooking a treat. The stairs to the second floor wrap around the fireplace and take the homeowners to the master bedroom and loft area.

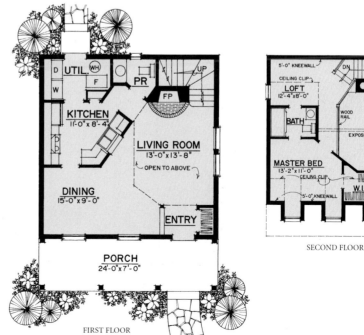

SECOND FLOOR

FIRST FLOOR

This two-story home's rustic design reflects thoughtful planning, including a porch that fully wraps the house in comfort and provides lots of room for rocking chairs. A stone chimney and arched windows set in dormers further enhance this home's country appeal. Inside, the floor plan is designed for maximum efficiency. A great room with a sloped ceiling enjoys a raised-hearth fireplace whose warmth radiates into the kitchen/nook. The master suite is located on the first floor and includes plenty of closet space and a private bath filled with amenities. A utility room and a powder room complete this level. The second floor contains two secondary bedrooms, a full bath, and a loft/study with a window seat.

plan# HPK1900059

First Floor: 1,093 sq. ft.
Second Floor: 603 sq. ft.
Total: 1,696 sq. ft.
Bedrooms: 3
Bathrooms: 2½
Width: 52' - 0"
Depth: 46' - 0"
Foundation: Crawlspace

ORDER ONLINE @ EPLANS.COM

FIRST FLOOR

SECOND FLOOR

ORDER BLUEPRINTS 24 HOURS, 7 DAYS A WEEK, AT 1-800-521-6797

© 1994 Donald A. Gardner Architects, Inc.

B. NATHAN

plan # HPK1900060

Square Footage: 2,207
Bonus Space: 435 sq. ft.
Bedrooms: 4
Bathrooms: 2½
Width: 76' - 1"
Depth: 50' - 0"

ORDER ONLINE @ EPLANS.COM

REAR EXTERIOR

This quaint four-bedroom home with front and rear porches reinforces its beauty with arched windows and dormers. The pillared dining room opens on the right, and a study that could double as a guest room is available on the left. Straight ahead lies the massive great room with its cathedral ceiling, enchanting fireplace, and access to the private rear porch. Within steps of the dining room is the efficient kitchen and the sunny breakfast nook. The master suite enjoys a cathedral ceiling, rear-deck access, and a master bath with a skylit whirlpool tub. Three additional bedrooms located at the opposite end of the house share a full bath.

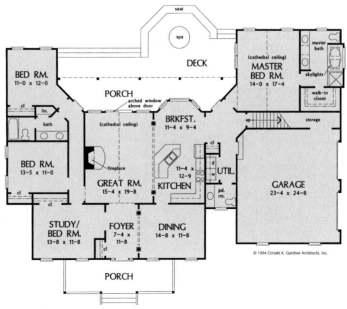

© 1994 Donald A. Gardner Architects, Inc.

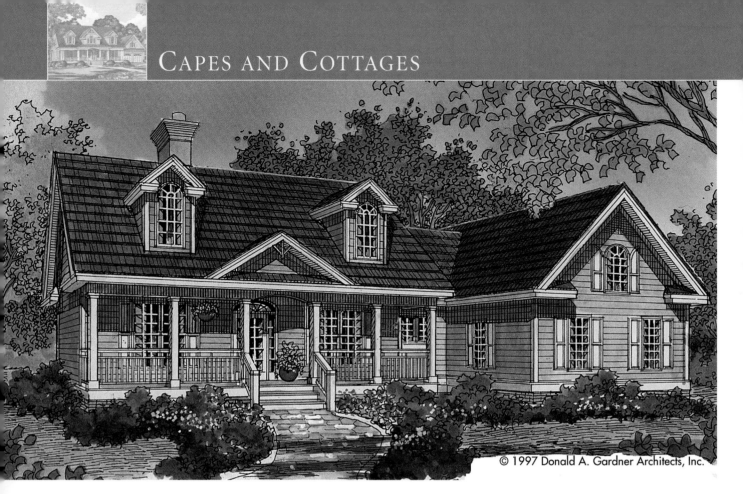

© 1997 Donald A. Gardner Architects, Inc.

A classic country exterior enriches the appearance of this economical home. A grand front porch and two skylit back porches encourage weekend relaxation. The great room features a cathedral ceiling and a fireplace with adjacent built-ins. The master suite enjoys a double-door entry, back-porch access, and a tray ceiling. The master bath has a garden tub set in the corner, a separate shower, twin vanities, and a skylight. Loads of storage, an open floor plan, and walls of windows make this three-bedroom plan very livable.

plan# HPK1900061

Square Footage: 1,652
Bonus Space: 367 sq. ft.
Bedrooms: 3
Bathrooms: 2
Width: 64' - 4"
Depth: 51' - 0"

ORDER ONLINE @ EPLANS.COM

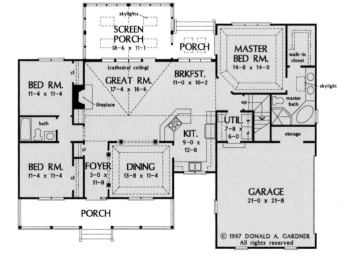

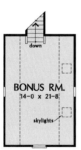

© 1997 DONALD A. GARDNER
All rights reserved

© 1995 Donald A. Gardner Architects, Inc.

plan # HPK1900062

Square Footage: 2,192
Bonus Space: 390 sq. ft.
Bedrooms: 4
Bathrooms: 2½
Width: 74' - 10"
Depth: 55' - 8"

ORDER ONLINE @ EPLANS.COM

REAR EXTERIOR

Exciting volumes and nine-foot ceilings add elegance to this comfortable, open plan. Hosts whose guests always end up in the kitchen will enjoy entertaining here, with only columns separating it from the great room. Children's bedrooms share a full bath that's complete with a linen closet. The master suite, located in a quiet wing, is highlighted by a tray ceiling and includes a skylit bath with a garden tub, private toilet, double-bowl vanity, and spacious walk-in closet.

©1995 Donald A. Gardner Architects, Inc.

© 1993 Donald A. Gardner Architects, Inc.

B. NATHAN.

Meandering through this four-bedroom farmhouse with its wraparound porch, you'll find country living at its best. A front Palladian dormer window and rear clerestory windows in the great room add exciting visual elements to the exterior and provide natural light to the interior. The large great room boasts a fireplace, bookshelves, and a raised cathedral ceiling, allowing a curved balcony overlook above. The great room, master bedroom, and breakfast room are accessible to the rear porch for greater circulation and flexibility. Special features such as the large cooktop island in the kitchen, the wet bar, the bedroom/study, the generous bonus room over the garage, and ample storage space set this plan apart.

plan # HPK1900063

First Floor: 2,064 sq. ft.
Second Floor: 594 sq. ft.
Total: 2,658 sq. ft.
Bonus Space: 483 sq. ft.
Bedrooms: 4
Bathrooms: 3½
Width: 92' - 0"
Depth: 57' - 8"

ORDER ONLINE @ EPLANS.COM

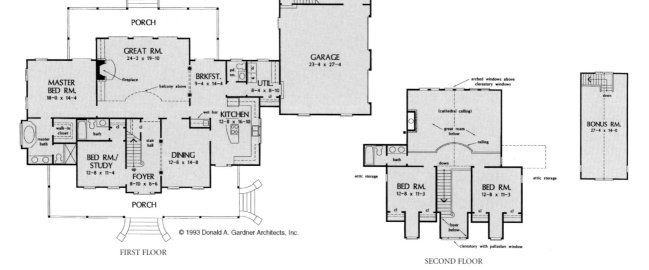

© 1993 Donald A. Gardner Architects, Inc.

FIRST FLOOR

SECOND FLOOR

ORDER BLUEPRINTS 24 HOURS, 7 DAYS A WEEK, AT 1-800-521-6797

© 1994 Donald A. Gardner Architects, Inc.

plan# HPK1900064

First Floor: 1,841 sq. ft.
Second Floor: 594 sq. ft.
Total: 2,435 sq. ft.
Bonus Space: 391 sq. ft.
Bedrooms: 4
Bathrooms: 3
Width: 82' - 2"
Depth: 48' - 10"

ORDER ONLINE @ EPLANS.COM

REAR EXTERIOR

© 1994 Donald A. Gardner Architects, Inc.

Spaciousness and lots of amenities earmark this design as a family favorite. The front wraparound porch leads to the foyer where a bedroom/study and dining room open. The central great room presents a warming fireplace, a two-story cathedral ceiling, and access to the rear porch. The kitchen features an island food-prep counter and opens to a bayed breakfast area, which conveniently accesses the garage through a side utility room. In the master suite, a private bath with a bumped-out tub and a walk-in closet are extra enhancements. Upstairs, two bedrooms flank a full bath. A bonus room over the garage allows for future expansion.

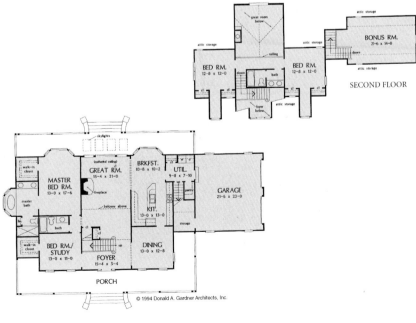

SECOND FLOOR

FIRST FLOOR

© 1994 Donald A. Gardner Architects, Inc.

© 1993 Donald A. Gardner Architects, Inc.

The foyer and great room in this magnificent farmhouse have Palladian window clerestories to allow natural light to enter, illuminating the whole house. The spacious great room boasts a fireplace, cabinets, and bookshelves. The second-floor balcony overlooks the great room. The kitchen with a cooking island is conveniently located between the dining room and the breakfast room with an open view of the great room. A generous master bedroom has plenty of closet space as well as an expansive master bath. A bonus room over the garage allows for expansion.

plan# HPK1900065

First Floor: 1,618 sq. ft.
Second Floor: 570 sq. ft.
Total: 2,188 sq. ft.
Bonus Space: 495 sq. ft.
Bedrooms: 3
Bathrooms: 2½
Width: 87' - 0"
Depth: 57' - 0"

ORDER ONLINE @ EPLANS.COM

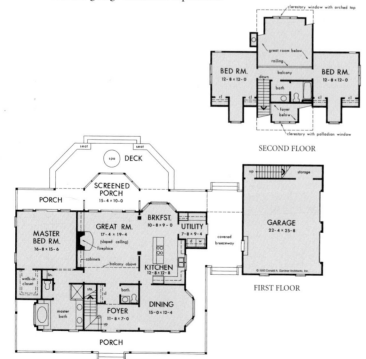

©1998 Donald A. Gardner, Inc.

plan# HPK1900066

First Floor: 1,569 sq. ft.
Second Floor: 682 sq. ft.
Total: 2,251 sq. ft.
Bonus Space: 332 sq. ft.
Bedrooms: 3
Bathrooms: 2½
Width: 64' - 8"
Depth: 43' - 4"

ORDER ONLINE @ EPLANS.COM

The wide porch across the front and the deck off the great room in back allow as much outdoor living as the weather permits. The foyer opens through columns from the front porch to the dining room, with a nearby powder room, and to the great room. The breakfast room is open to the great room and the adjacent kitchen. The utility room adjoins this area and accesses the garage. On the opposite side of the plan, the master suite offers a compartmented bath and two walk-in closets. A staircase leads upstairs to two family bedrooms—one at each end of a balcony that overlooks the great room. Each bedroom contains a walk-in closet, a dormer window, and private access to the bath through a private vanity area.

FIRST FLOOR

SECOND FLOOR

© 2003 Donald A. Gardner, Inc.

Circle-head transoms and decorative brackets soften strong angled gables, and bold columns define a welcoming country porch. Service entries from the garage, deck, and utility/mudroom create convenience. Inside, a curved balcony separates the two-story foyer and great room, which is marked by columns at the entrance and warmed by a fireplace. A bay window extends the breakfast nook that is adjacent to the kitchen. The first-floor master suite is well appointed, and the master bath is complete with a dual-sink vanity, separate tub and shower, and nearby walk-in closets. Both second-floor bedrooms have their own private baths. This home is equipped with a bonus room, and outdoor living space is abundant.

plan# HPK1900067

First Floor: 1,848 sq. ft.
Second Floor: 799 sq. ft.
Total: 2,647 sq. ft.
Bonus Space: 457 sq. ft.
Bedrooms: 3
Bathrooms: 3½
Width: 81' - 0"
Depth: 49' - 8"

ORDER ONLINE @ EPLANS.COM

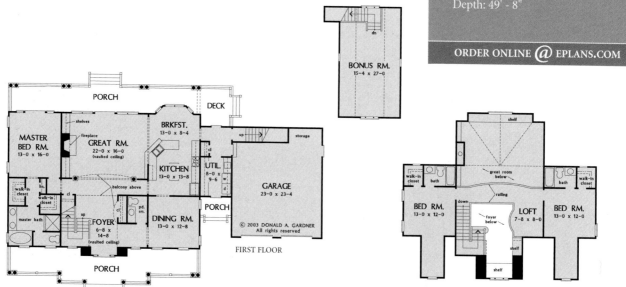

CLASSIC FARMHOUSES

PHOTO COURTESY OF THE MCGUIRE GROUP ARCHITECTS

D rive along a country road or rural highway and at least one farmhouse will be clearly visible from the car. Stretching across America's landscape, this classic style has a way of blending with its surroundings yet standing out, adding beauty to a backdrop of corn fields or suburban lawns.

The two-story farmhouse dates back to the colonial Victorian era, but current designs evolved to include elements from many architectural styles. Greek Revival design appears in the columns along the front porch. Widow's walks and romantic balconies originate in the Colonial styles of southern plantations. The flared eaves of roof overhangs come from the Dutch Colonial designs of the 17th and 18th Centuries. The founding Victorian influence brings turrets and scrolling brackets to porches and windows.

More vertical in shape than the preceding capes and cottages, the classic farmhouse was made to suit a growing family, with several upstairs bedrooms and a kitchen with outdoor access through either a porch or garage. The covered front porch, a staple in American farmhouses, protected the home from weather damage and provided a space for outdoor summer living during a time when central air conditioning was a dream of the future. An often central fireplace had a much easier time heating the small vertical footprint of the farmhouse during the cold winter months.

While these homes were once the utilitarian dwelling places of hardworking farmers, they now can also be a family's lap of luxury in a residential community; the tall design makes these homes perfectly suited for narrow lots. Today, many plans include dormers, which increase second-floor living space, and the convenience of a downstairs master bedroom, which makes the home a worthwhile investment that will endure for many years.

A simple and familiar elevation is the best attribute of this home. See more on page 89.

PHOTO COURTESY OF DRUMMOND DESIGNS, INC.

This lovely country design features a stunning wrapping porch and plenty of windows to provide the interior with natural light. The living room boasts a centered fireplace that helps to define this spacious open area. A nine-foot ceiling on the first floor adds a sense of spaciousness and light. The casual living room leads outdoors to a rear porch. Upstairs, four bedrooms cluster around a central hall. The master suite sports a walk-in closet and a deluxe bath with an oval tub and a separate shower.

plan # HPK1900068

First Floor: 1,060 sq. ft.
Second Floor: 1,039 sq. ft.
Total: 2,099 sq. ft.
Bedrooms: 4
Bathrooms: 2½
Width: 50' - 8"
Depth: 39' - 4"
Foundation: Unfinished Basement

ORDER ONLINE @ EPLANS.COM

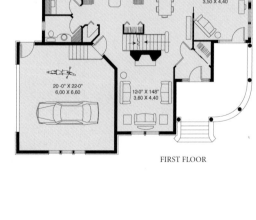

FIRST FLOOR

SECOND FLOOR

ORDER BLUEPRINTS 24 HOURS, 7 DAYS A WEEK, AT 1-800-521-6797

FOR MORE DETAILED INFORMATION, PLEASE CHECK THE FLOOR PLANS CAREFULLY.

plan# HPK1900069

First Floor: 1,804 sq. ft.
Second Floor: 1,041 sq. ft.
Total: 2,845 sq. ft.
Bedrooms: 4
Bathrooms: 3½
Width: 57' - 3"
Depth: 71' - 0"
Foundation: Finished Walkout Basement

ORDER ONLINE @ EPLANS.COM

There's a feeling of old Charleston in this stately home—particularly on the quiet side porch that wraps around the kitchen and breakfast room. The interior of this home revolves around a spacious great room with a welcoming fireplace. The left wing is dedicated to the master suite, which boasts wide views of the rear property. A corner kitchen easily serves planned events in the formal dining room, as well as family meals in the breakfast area. Three family bedrooms, one with a private bath and the others sharing a bath, are tucked upstairs.

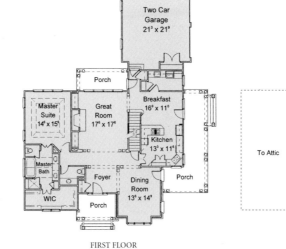

FIRST FLOOR

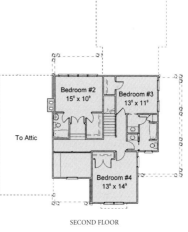

SECOND FLOOR

PHOTOGRAPHY PROVIDED BY STEPHEN FULLER, INC.

The covered front stoop of this two-story, traditionally styled home gives way to the foyer and formal areas inside. A cozy living room with a fireplace sits on the right, and an elongated dining room is on the left. For fine family living, a great room and a kitchen/breakfast area account for the rear of the first-floor plan. A guest room with a nearby full bath finishes off the accommodations. Upstairs, four bedrooms include a master suite fit for royalty. A bonus room rests near Bedroom 2 and would make a great office or additional bedroom.

plan# HPK1900070

First Floor: 1,700 sq. ft.
Second Floor: 1,585 sq. ft.
Total: 3,285 sq. ft.
Bonus Space: 176 sq. ft.
Bedrooms: 5
Bathrooms: 4
Width: 60' - 0"
Depth: 47' - 6"
Foundation: Finished Walkout Basement

ORDER ONLINE @ EPLANS.COM

FIRST FLOOR

SECOND FLOOR

ORDER BLUEPRINTS 24 HOURS, 7 DAYS A WEEK, AT 1-800-521-6797

FOR MORE DETAILED INFORMATION, PLEASE CHECK THE FLOOR PLANS CAREFULLY.

plan # HPK1900071

First Floor: 1,368 sq. ft.
Second Floor: 1,140 sq. ft.
Total: 2,508 sq. ft.
Bedrooms: 4
Bathrooms: 2½
Width: 62' - 0"
Depth: 48' - 0"
Foundation: Unfinished Basement

ORDER ONLINE @ EPLANS.COM

Three dormers on a side-gabled roof and classic fenestration establish a pleasing Colonial style to this home's facade. The attention to the entryway and second-floor balcony are finer touches owners will appreciate. The interior offers an uncomplicated layout—gathering spaces on the lower floor and sleeping quarters above. The family room enjoys a majestic fireplace and incredible views through the intimate bay window. The family room, dinette, and kitchen form one large area, with direct access from kitchen to formal dining room. A handy large closet and laundry are also accessible from the kitchen.

SECOND FLOOR

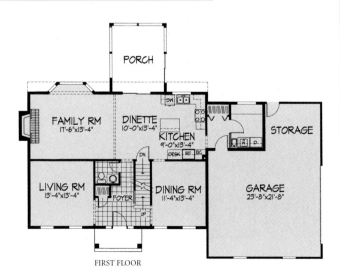

FIRST FLOOR

CHRIS A. LITTLE FROM ATLANTA; COURTESY OF CHATHAM HOME PLANNING, INC.

The standing-seam metal roof adds character to this four- (or five-) bedroom home. The covered front porch, screened porch, and rear deck add outdoor living spaces for nature enthusiasts. A flexible room is found to the left of the foyer and the dining room is to the right. The galley kitchen is accessed through an archway with a sunny breakfast nook adjoining at the back. The lavish master suite is on the left with a private bath that includes access to the laundry room. The second floor holds three bedrooms and a multimedia room where the family can spend quality time in a casual atmosphere.

plan # HPK1900072

First Floor: 2,036 sq. ft.
Second Floor: 1,230 sq. ft.
Total: 3,266 sq. ft.
Bedrooms: 4
Bathrooms: 3½
Width: 57' - 4"
Depth: 59' - 0"
Foundation: Pier (same as Piling)

ORDER ONLINE @ EPLANS.COM

FIRST FLOOR

Wood Deck
29'3"x 10'

Screen Porch
28'5"x 8'

Master Bedroom
15'5"x 15'6"

Breakfast
11'4"x 17'6"

Living Room
22'x 16'6"

Kitchen

Study/
Bedroom
12'8"x11'

Foyer

Dining
12'8"x 12'8"

Porch
47'x 12'

SECOND FLOOR

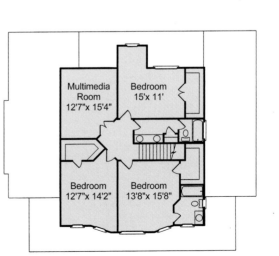

Multimedia
Room
12'7"x 15'4"

Bedroom
15'x 11'

Bedroom
12'7"x 14'2"

Bedroom
13'8"x 15'8"

FIRST FLOOR

SECOND FLOOR

FOR MORE DETAILED INFORMATION, PLEASE CHECK THE FLOOR PLANS CAREFULLY.

plan# HPK1900073

First Floor: 1,706 sq. ft.
Second Floor: 1,123 sq. ft.
Total: 2,829 sq. ft.
Bedrooms: 3
Bathrooms: 2½
Width: 71' - 2"
Depth: 64' - 6"
Foundation: Crawlspace

ORDER ONLINE @ EPLANS.COM

Plentiful outdoor living spaces make this an ideal home for entertaining. Inside, the open floor plan allows easy interaction between rooms. The spacious island kitchen conveniently serves the family room and dining room. At the rear of the first floor, a fireplace warms the living room. Upstairs houses the master bedroom, outfitted with tray ceilings, a dual-sink vanity, a garden tub and separate shower, and a compartmented toilet. The adjacent home office is an added convenience. Two additional family bedrooms share a full bath. A three-car garage completes this plan.

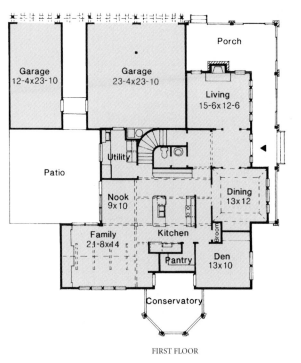

FIRST FLOOR

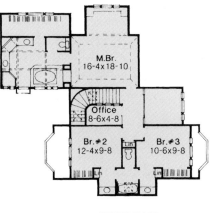

SECOND FLOOR

Covered porches, front and back, are a fine preview to the livable nature of this Victorian home. Living areas are defined in a family room with a fireplace, formal living and dining rooms, and a kitchen with a breakfast room. An ample laundry room, a garage with a storage area, and a powder room round out the first floor. Three second-floor bedrooms are joined by a study and two full baths. The master suite on this floor has two closets, including an ample walk-in, as well as a relaxing bath with a tile-rimmed whirlpool tub and a separate shower with a seat.

plan# HPK1900074

First Floor: 1,375 sq. ft.
Second Floor: 1,016 sq. ft.
Total: 2,391 sq. ft.
Bedrooms: 3
Bathrooms: 2½
Width: 62' - 7"
Depth: 54' - 0"
Foundation: Unfinished Basement

ORDER ONLINE @ EPLANS.COM

FIRST FLOOR

SECOND FLOOR

THIS HOME, AS SHOWN IN THE PHOTOGRAPH, MAY DIFFER FROM THE ACTUAL BLUEPRINTS. FOR MORE DETAILED INFORMATION, PLEASE CHECK THE FLOOR PLANS CAREFULLY.

plan# HPK1900075

First Floor: 1,156 sq. ft.
Second Floor: 988 sq. ft.
Total: 2,144 sq. ft.
Bedrooms: 4
Bathrooms: 2½
Width: 70' - 0"
Depth: 60' - 0"
Foundation: Unfinished Basement

ORDER ONLINE @ EPLANS.COM

A wraparound porch and symmetrical facade effect a warm curbside presence for this country-style two-story. Inside, an uncomplicated layout establishes shared spaces on the first floor—including a family room with fireplace—and sleeping quarters on the second floor. The living and dining rooms each enjoy views toward the front of the house. The family room, dinette, and kitchen share one expansive space. The master suite is accompanied by a generous walk-in closet and full bath. The remaining three bedrooms share a full bath among them.

FIRST FLOOR

SECOND FLOOR

PHOTOGRAPHS: ©BRAD OWEN, ASHEVILLE, NC, BILL GRANT DESIGNER, LLC

The wraparound porch extends a warm welcome to family and friends alike. Inside, the study and dining room flank the foyer. Straight ahead, the family room, enhanced by a tray ceiling, is warmed by a fireplace on the left wall. The master bedroom, family room, and breakfast area each enjoy a private entrance to the rear porch. Upstairs houses three additional family bedrooms, three full baths, and a bonus room. A three-car garage completes this plan.

plan# HPK1900076

First Floor: 2,524 sq. ft.
Second Floor: 1,326 sq. ft.
Total: 3,850 sq. ft.
Bonus Space: 723 sq. ft.
Bedrooms: 4
Bathrooms: 4½
Width: 107' - 7"
Depth: 58' - 7"
Foundation: Unfinished Basement

ORDER ONLINE @ EPLANS.COM

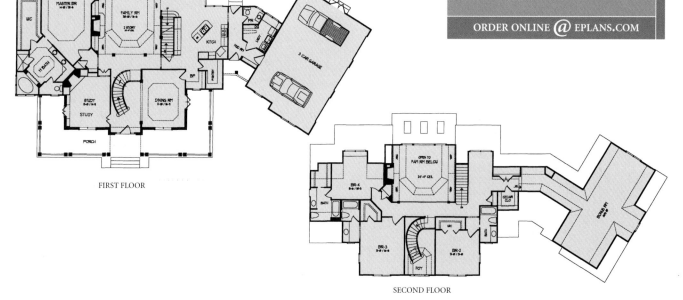

FIRST FLOOR

SECOND FLOOR

FOR MORE DETAILED INFORMATION, PLEASE CHECK THE FLOOR PLANS CAREFULLY.

plan# HPK1900077

First Floor: 1,250 sq. ft.

Second Floor: 1,166 sq. ft.

Total: 2,416 sq. ft.

Bedrooms: 4

Bathrooms: 2½

Width: 64' - 0"

Depth: 52' - 0"

Foundation: Unfinished Walkout Basement

ORDER ONLINE @ EPLANS.COM

With its classic features, this home is reminiscent of Main Street, USA. The two-story foyer is flanked by the formal living and dining rooms, and the stairs are tucked back in the center of the house. Columns create a separation from the family room to the breakfast area, keeping that open feeling across the entire rear of the house. Corner windows in the kitchen look into the side yard and rear screened porch. The porch leads to the rear deck, which also ties into the side porch, creating outdoor living on three sides of the house. As you ascend the staircase to the second floor, you will pass a lighted panel of stained glass on the landing, creating the illusion of a window wall. The second floor features four bedrooms and a compartmented hall bath.

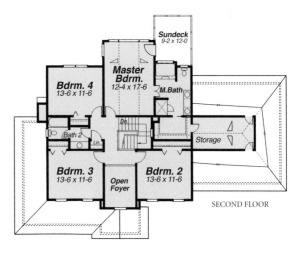

SECOND FLOOR

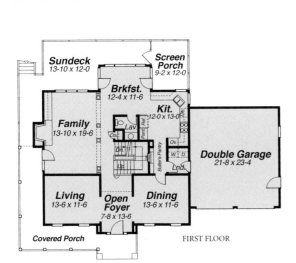

FIRST FLOOR

This sweet facade pays homage to the architectural symmetry of simpler times. A deep front porch welcomes guests and complements a triplet of charming windows. Inside, formal rooms frame the foyer, which provides a discreet staircase. The kitchen is enhanced by an island snackbar and access to the rear breezeway. The family room is open to the kitchen and is warmed by a central fireplace. Upstairs, two secondary bedrooms have plenty of closet space and share a full bath. The master suite features two walk-in closets, a double-bowl vanity, and a separate shower and tub. A garage is placed to the rear of the plan.

plan # HPK1900078

First Floor: 1,041 sq. ft.
Second Floor: 998 sq. ft.
Total: 2,039 sq. ft.
Bonus Space: 381 sq. ft.
Bedrooms: 3
Bathrooms: 2½
Width: 44' - 10"
Depth: 84' - 6"
Foundation: Slab

ORDER ONLINE @ EPLANS.COM

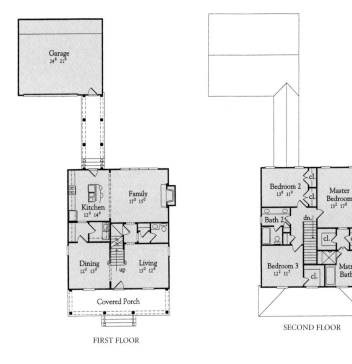

Garage
24⁸ 21⁰

Kitchen
12⁰ 14⁶

Family
17⁰ 15⁰

Dining
12⁰ 13⁰

Living
13⁰ 12⁶

up

Covered Porch

FIRST FLOOR

Bedroom 2
13⁸ 11⁰

Master Bedroom
13² 17⁰

Bath 2

dn.

cl.

cl.

cl.

cl.

Bedroom 3
12¹ 11⁷

Mstr. Bath

cl.

SECOND FLOOR

THIS HOME, AS SHOWN, MAY DIFFER FROM THE ACTUAL BLUEPRINTS. FOR MORE DETAILED INFORMATION, PLEASE CHECK THE FLOOR PLANS CAREFULLY.

plan# HPK1900079

First Floor: 832 sq. ft.
Second Floor: 789 sq. ft.
Total: 1,621 sq. ft.
Bedrooms: 3
Bathrooms: 2½
Width: 44' - 0"
Depth: 32' - 0"
Foundation: Crawlspace, Unfinished Basement

ORDER ONLINE @ EPLANS.COM

A wraparound porch introduces this practical design that's full of amenities. Windows open up the living room on three sides to let in natural light and let you keep an eye on kids playing on the porch. The U-shaped kitchen opens to the bright breakfast room. A spacious dining room and a powder room complete the first floor. The second floor offers the master suite—with a walk-in closet and private bath—and two family bedrooms that share a hall bath.

SECOND FLOOR

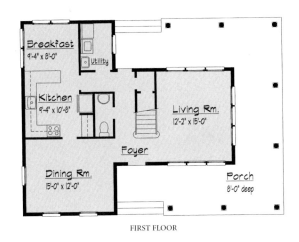

FIRST FLOOR

©1993 DONALD A. GARDNER ARCHITECTS, INC., PHOTOGRAPHY COURTESY OF DONALD A. GARDNER ARCHITECTS, INC.

Three dormers top a very welcoming covered wraparound porch on this attractive country home. The entrance enjoys a Palladian clerestory window, letting an abundance of natural light into the foyer. The great room furthers this feeling of airiness with a balcony above and two sets of sliding glass doors leading to the back porch. For privacy, the master suite occupies the right side of the first floor. With a sitting bay and all the amenities of a modern master bath, this lavish retreat will be a welcome haven for the homeowner. Two family bedrooms reside upstairs, sharing a balcony overlook into the great room.

plan# HPK1900080

First Floor: 2,316 sq. ft.
Second Floor: 721 sq. ft.
Total: 3,037 sq. ft.
Bonus Space: 545 sq. ft.
Bedrooms: 4
Bathrooms: 3½
Width: 95' - 4"
Depth: 54' - 10"

ORDER ONLINE @ EPLANS.COM

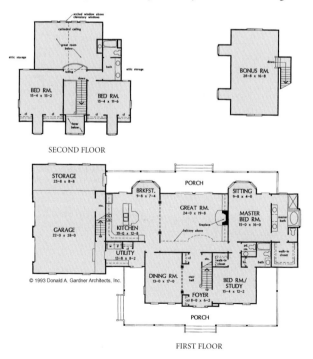

SECOND FLOOR

FIRST FLOOR

© 1993 Donald A. Gardner Architects, Inc.

ORDER BLUEPRINTS 24 HOURS, 7 DAYS A WEEK, AT 1-800-521-6797

plan# HPK1900081

First Floor: 831 sq. ft.
Second Floor: 791 sq. ft.
Total: 1,622 sq. ft.
Bedrooms: 3
Bathrooms: 2½
Width: 28' - 8"
Depth: 32' - 8"
Foundation: Unfinished Basement

ORDER ONLINE @ EPLANS.COM

A classic cross-gabled design and full-length porch lend country charm to this compact home. Inside, wide open spaces for gathering and dining encircle the center stair. An L-shaped kitchen wraps around a central island with cooktop and casual seating. A rear entry off the kitchen gives access to the porch and backyard. Completing the lower level, a compartmented utility room puts laundry, pantry, and powder room at your convenience. Upstairs, the efficient layout provides space for a master suite with all the amenities, and two additional bedrooms that share a bath.

FIRST FLOOR

SECOND FLOOR

This beautiful three-bedroom home boasts many attractive features. Two covered porches will entice you outside; inside, a special sunroom on the first floor brings the outdoors in. The foyer opens on the right to a comfortable family room that may be used as a home office. On the left, the living area is warmed by the sunroom and a cozy corner fireplace. A formal dining area lies adjacent to an efficient kitchen with a central island and breakfast nook overlooking the back porch. The second level offers two family bedrooms served by a full bath. A spacious master suite with a walk-in closet and luxurious bath completes the second floor.

plan# HPK1900082

First Floor: 1,232 sq. ft.
Second Floor: 951 sq. ft.
Total: 2,183 sq. ft.
Bonus Space: 365 sq. ft.
Bedrooms: 3
Bathrooms: 2½
Width: 56' - 0"
Depth: 38' - 0"
Foundation: Unfinished Basement

SEARCH ONLINE @ EPLANS.COM

FIRST FLOOR

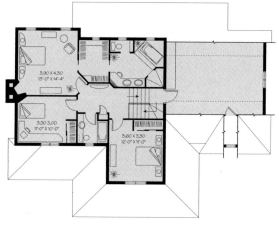

SECOND FLOOR

plan # HPK1900083

First Floor: 694 sq. ft.

Second Floor: 558 sq. ft.

Total: 1,252 sq. ft.

Bedrooms: 2

Bathrooms: 1½

Width: 28' - 0"

Depth: 40' - 0"

Foundation: Unfinished Basement

ORDER ONLINE @ EPLANS.COM

A glass-door entrance welcomes visitors into the picturesque charm of this countryside home. A large wraparound porch leads to a relaxing outdoor lounge area—perfect for summer afternoons. The island kitchen opens to an eating area across from the living room. A powder room, laundry area, and the one-car garage complete this floor. Upstairs, two family bedrooms are linked by a full bath.

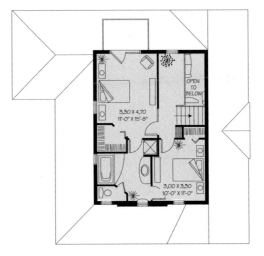

SECOND FLOOR

FIRST FLOOR

Traditional style doesn't have to mean ordinary, as this country home beautifully proves. Enter through French doors to the elegant foyer, spacious enough for a small chair and entry table. This area also serves as a functional mudroom as you continue to the bright, airy family room. Ample space in the kitchen accommodates multiple cooks, and formal or casual dining options suit any occasion. Bedrooms are located upstairs, along with a majestic spa bath.

plan# HPK1900084

First Floor: 756 sq. ft.
Second Floor: 676 sq. ft.
Total: 1,432 sq. ft.
Bedrooms: 3
Bathrooms: 2
Width: 38' - 8"
Depth: 32' - 0"
Foundation: Unfinished Basement

ORDER ONLINE @ EPLANS.COM

FIRST FLOOR

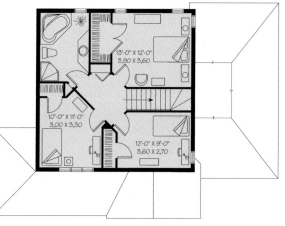

SECOND FLOOR

plan# HPK1900085

First Floor: 860 sq. ft.
Second Floor: 840 sq. ft.
Total: 1,700 sq. ft.
Bedrooms: 3
Bathrooms: 1½
Width: 30' - 0"
Depth: 29' - 0"
Foundation: Unfinished Basement

ORDER ONLINE @ EPLANS.COM

The wraparound front porch welcomes you home to this classic country farmhouse design. Two floors of family-friendly space await inside. The first level is devoted to living spaces. An island kitchen with plenty of space for helping hands has direct access to both a formal dining room and an informal niche backed by a wall of windows with views to the rear yard. Assemble the kids and some friends in the great room for a movie or a board game. Three bedrooms are situated upstairs, including the master bedroom with a large walk-in closet. The bathroom is shared by all rooms and has a dual-sink vanity, separate tub and shower, and plenty of space.

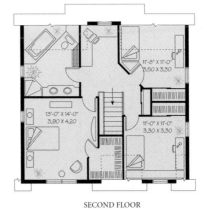

SECOND FLOOR

FIRST FLOOR

Economy and style are key in this delightful Victorian-flavored home. A wraparound porch offers protection from the elements and adds substantially to the living space while a faux balcony and oval window lend character. The intimate living room creates a warm and friendly impression just inside the enclosed entry. Here, a grand staircase leads to a second-floor computer nook and three bedrooms that share an elaborate full bath. Returning to the first floor, the formal dining room adjoins the kitchen and breakfast area.

plan# HPK1900086

First Floor: 802 sq. ft.
Second Floor: 802 sq. ft.
Total: 1,604 sq. ft.
Bedrooms: 3
Bathrooms: 1½
Width: 28' - 0"
Depth: 32' - 0"
Foundation: Unfinished Basement

ORDER ONLINE @ EPLANS.COM

FIRST FLOOR

SECOND FLOOR

plan # HPK1900087

First Floor: 808 sq. ft.
Second Floor: 808 sq. ft.
Total: 1,616 sq. ft.
Bedrooms: 3
Bathrooms: 1½
Width: 45' - 0"
Depth: 32' - 0"
Foundation: Unfinished Basement

ORDER ONLINE @ EPLANS.COM

Victorian detailing inspires memories of holidays at the family farm. Imagine the gables and eaves dripping with icicles. Inside, an enclosed foyer keeps the cold wind out and provides a place to leave muddy boots. A formal dining room hosts a feast, served up by a gaggle of family chefs from the spacious kitchen. If you're staying the night, there are three bedrooms to choose from, with a bath big enough for all to share.

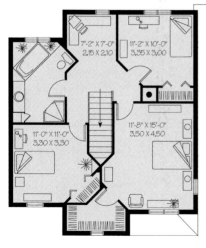

SECOND FLOOR

FIRST FLOOR

Keystones and shutters accent the brick facade of this charming country home. First-floor living space consists of a living room, dining area, and kitchen; the utility room and a full bath are nearby. A snack bar in the kitchen provides convenient service to the adjoining breakfast nook. Upstairs, two family bedrooms share another full bath with the spacious master bedroom.

plan# HPK1900088

First Floor: 754 sq. ft.
Second Floor: 744 sq. ft.
Total: 1,498 sq. ft.
Bedrooms: 3
Bathrooms: 2
Width: 32' - 0"
Depth: 36' - 0"
Foundation: Unfinished Basement

ORDER ONLINE @ EPLANS.COM

FIRST FLOOR

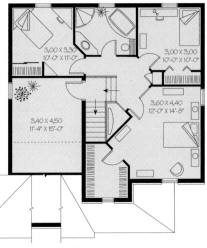

SECOND FLOOR

ORDER BLUEPRINTS 24 HOURS, 7 DAYS A WEEK, AT 1-800-521-6797

plan # HPK1900089

First Floor: 960 sq. ft.
Second Floor: 838 sq. ft.
Total: 1,798 sq. ft.
Bedrooms: 3
Bathrooms: 1½
Width: 36' - 0"
Depth: 30' - 0"
Foundation: Unfinished Basement

ORDER ONLINE @ EPLANS.COM

This romantic cottage design is ideal for any countryside setting. Lively Victorian details enhance the exterior. A wrapping porch with a gazebo-style sitting area encourages refreshing outdoor relaxation; interior spaces are open to each other. The kitchen with a snack bar is open to both the dining area and the living room. A powder bath with laundry facilities completes the first floor. The second floor offers space for three family bedrooms with walk-in closets and a pampering whirlpool bath.

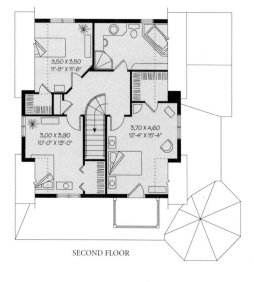

SECOND FLOOR

FIRST FLOOR

Here's a charmer for the growing family. Front and rear covered porches and three bedrooms, with space for a fourth, highlight this magnificent plan. The main living areas—dining room, living room, and den—flow together offering great versatility in how they are organized and used. The kitchen is joined to the rear breakfast alcove by a counter. It opens to the garage through the laundry room where a bench makes it easier to take off muddy or wet foot gear before entering the house. Upstairs, two bedrooms share a bath and a linen closet, and the master suite enjoys many special comforts. A hallway connects to extra space over the garage.

plan# HPK1900090

First Floor: 954 sq. ft.
Second Floor: 783 sq. ft.
Total: 1,737 sq. ft.
Bonus Space: 327 sq. ft.
Bedrooms: 3
Bathrooms: 2½
Width: 56' - 0"
Depth: 40' - 0"
Foundation: Crawlspace

ORDER ONLINE @ EPLANS.COM

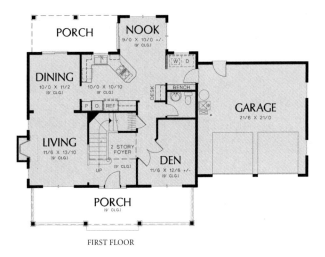

FIRST FLOOR

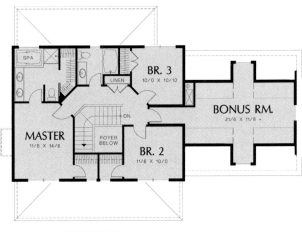

SECOND FLOOR

plan # HPK1900091

First Floor: 1,319 sq. ft.
Second Floor: 1,181 sq. ft.
Total: 2,500 sq. ft.
Bonus Space: 371 sq. ft.
Bedrooms: 4
Bathrooms: 2½
Width: 60' - 0"
Depth: 42' - 0"
Foundation: Crawlspace

ORDER ONLINE @ EPLANS.COM

A stunning shingle home with stone accents (including a stone fireplace!), this Cape Cod-style home will complement any neighborhood. Inside, the two-story foyer presents a grand staircase and high ceilings throughout. Multipane windows light up the living room; an archway connects it to the family room. Here, a lateral fireplace allows rear views. The breakfast nook has French doors to the rear property, inviting outdoor dining. The island kitchen is designed with lots of extra space to accommodate two cooks. A butler's pantry makes entertaining a breeze. Upstairs, three bedrooms (or make one a den) share a full bath and a bonus room. The master suite is graced with a vaulted ceiling and a private bath with a Roman spa tub.

SECOND FLOOR

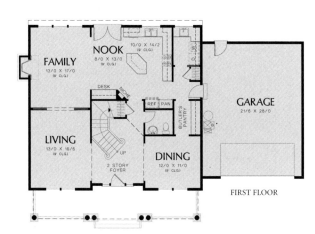

FIRST FLOOR

A wraparound covered porch and symmetrical dormers produce an inviting appearance to this farmhouse. Inside, the two-story foyer leads directly to the large great room graced by a fireplace and an abundance of windows. The U-shaped island kitchen is convenient to the sunny dining room with a powder room nearby. The utility room offers access to the two-car garage. Upstairs, two family bedrooms share a full hall bath and have convenient access to a large bonus room. The master suite is full of amenities, including a walk-in closet and a pampering bath. A bonus room is also available upstairs near the hall bath.

plan # HPK1900092

First Floor: 1,032 sq. ft.
Second Floor: 870 sq. ft.
Total: 1,902 sq. ft.
Bonus Space: 306 sq. ft.
Bedrooms: 3
Bathrooms: 2½
Width: 66' - 0"
Depth: 38' - 0"
Foundation: Crawlspace

ORDER ONLINE @ EPLANS.COM

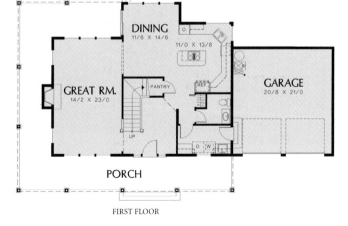

FIRST FLOOR

SECOND FLOOR

plan# HPK1900093

First Floor: 1,352 sq. ft.
Second Floor: 605 sq. ft.
Total: 1,957 sq. ft.
Bonus Space: 285 sq. ft.
Bedrooms: 3
Bathrooms: 2½
Width: 60' - 0"
Depth: 43' - 0"
Foundation: Crawlspace

ORDER ONLINE @ EPLANS.COM

The casual living space of this three-bedroom home is serenely comfortable, with flexible open spaces and stylish amenities. A soaring two-story great room has a fireplace and access to the outdoors. The morning nook enjoys the glow of the great room fireplace and is easily served by the angled kitchen. French doors lead to a secluded master suite with a U-shaped walk-in closet and an oversized shower. Upstairs, two family bedrooms share a hall bath with a double-bowl vanity.

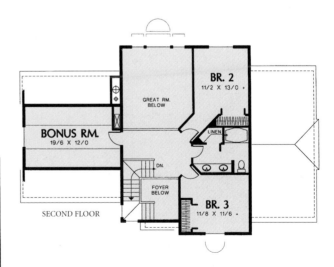

SECOND FLOOR

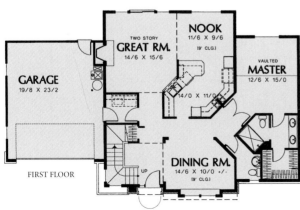

FIRST FLOOR

This plan says "welcome home," as Craftsman details make a warm entry. The view from the front door to the family room's two-story fireplace wall is amazing. The garage entry brings you past a home office that can easily be used as a guest bedroom. The expansive kitchen/breakfast area also features a command center—perfect for the family computer. A staircase leads to the second-floor balcony where three bedrooms share a bath. The master suite features a window seat on the back wall, dramatized by a stepped ceiling and large windows overlooking the back yard. An oversized master closet even has extra storage space that could be cedar-lined for those out-of-season clothes. The second-floor laundry and computer desk complete this well-appointed design.

plan# HPK1900094

First Floor: 1,315 sq. ft.
Second Floor: 1,380 sq. ft.
Total: 2,695 sq. ft.
Bedrooms: 5
Bathrooms: 3
Width: 50' - 0"
Depth: 44' - 0"
Foundation: Unfinished Walkout Basement

ORDER ONLINE @ EPLANS.COM

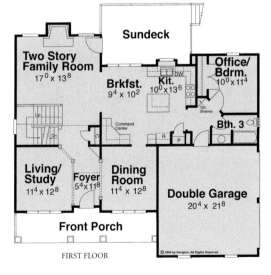

FIRST FLOOR

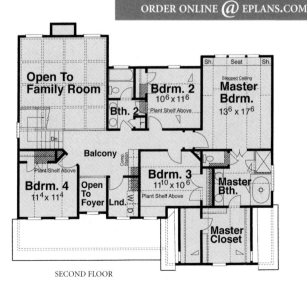

SECOND FLOOR

plan# HPK1900095

First Floor: 1,164 sq. ft.

Second Floor: 1,319 sq. ft.

Total: 2,483 sq. ft.

Bedrooms: 4

Bathrooms: 3

Width: 50' - 0"

Depth: 39' - 0"

Foundation: Unfinished Walkout Basement

ORDER ONLINE @ EPLANS.COM

This charming cottage offers more space than you might think. A two-story living area is seen from the foyer where the U-shaped staircase leads you upstairs. The spacious kitchen/breakfast room even allows for a command center—the perfect place for the family computer. The first-floor bedroom provides space for an unexpected guest or can double as a home office. The master suite offers the option of a dramatic ceiling treatment with windows overlooking the rear of the house. A closet beyond the master bath makes room for all your clothes while also providing low storage. The other bedrooms also boast dramatic ceiling treatments, creating a sense of spaciousness.

SECOND FLOOR

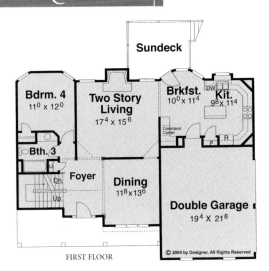

FIRST FLOOR

© 2004 by Designer, All Rights Reserved

Step into the two-story foyer, where a living room will greet you on the right and a boxed dining room on the left. Farther into the plan is a two-story family room with a corner fireplace. The kitchen looks over a bar into the bayed breakfast area, which has rear-door access to the sun deck. The first-floor master bedroom is situated at the rear of the plan for maximum privacy and includes many lavish amenities. The second level presents many unique additions for the whole family. A future media space is perfect for a home theater or perhaps an additional bedroom. Three family bedrooms and two full baths complete the sleeping quarters. A storage space, a loft, and overlooks to the two-story family room and foyer are included in this versatile design.

plan# HPK1900096

First Floor: 1,771 sq. ft.
Second Floor: 1,235 sq. ft.
Total: 3,006 sq. ft.
Bonus Space: 395 sq. ft.
Bedrooms: 4
Bathrooms: 3½
Width: 61' - 4"
Depth: 54' - 0"
Foundation: Crawlspace, Slab, Unfinished Walkout Basement

ORDER ONLINE @ EPLANS.COM

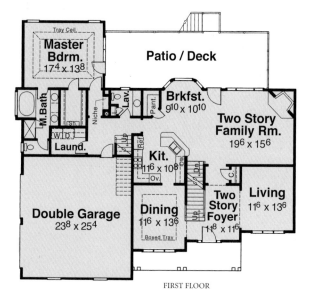

FIRST FLOOR

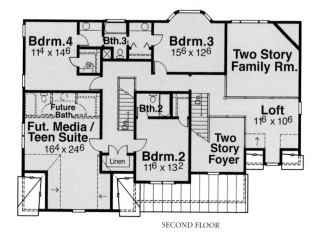

SECOND FLOOR

plan# HPK1900097

First Floor: 1,440 sq. ft.
Second Floor: 1,440 sq. ft.
Total: 2,880 sq. ft.
Bonus Space: 140 sq. ft.
Bedrooms: 4
Bathrooms: 2½
Width: 30' - 0"
Depth: 56' - 0"
Foundation: Unfinished Basement

ORDER ONLINE @ EPLANS.COM

The impressive exterior gives way to an interior without boundaries. The lack of unnecessary walls creates a feeling of spaciousness. Access to the sundeck from the family room extends the living space, encouraging entertaining. The second floor houses the master suite and three additional family bedrooms. Bedrooms 2 and 3 enjoy private access to a front-facing covered porch. A second-floor laundry room is an added convenience. The finished basement, boasting a sizable recreation room, completes this plan.

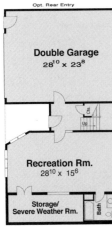

BASEMENT

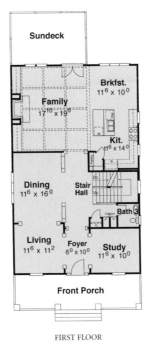

FIRST FLOOR

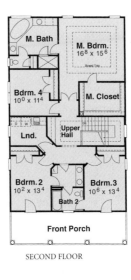

SECOND FLOOR

OPTIONAL LAYOUT

This romantic farmhouse, with its open living spaces, covered porches and decorative widow's walk, is designed with gracious family living in mind. From the lovely wraparound porch, the foyer first meets the front parlor through an arched doorway. The impressive formal dining room just beyond will be a delight for casual meals as well as formal affairs. The grand room takes center stage with rear-porch access, a corner fireplace, built-in media center and pass-through to the kitchen. The kitchen features a work island, eating counter and breakfast nook. The master suite is lavishly appointed with a spa-style bath, a sitting area and private access to the rear porch. Upstairs, a computer loft with built-ins serves as a common area to the three family bedrooms that share a full hall bath.

plan# HPK1900098

First Floor: 2,240 sq. ft.
Second Floor: 943 sq. ft.
Total: 3,183 sq. ft.
Bedrooms: 4
Bathrooms: 2½
Width: 69' - 8"
Depth: 61' - 10"
Foundation: Slab, Unfinished Basement

ORDER ONLINE @ EPLANS.COM

FIRST FLOOR

© THE SATER DESIGN COLLECTION, INC.

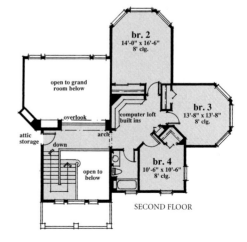

SECOND FLOOR

plan# HPK1900099

First Floor: 2,236 sq. ft.
Second Floor: 1,208 sq. ft.
Total: 3,444 sq. ft.
Bonus Space: 318 sq. ft.
Bedrooms: 4
Bathrooms: 4
Width: 42' - 6"
Depth: 71' - 4"
Foundation: Pier (same as Piling)

ORDER ONLINE @ EPLANS.COM

This spacious home offers a front porch and a second-floor balcony, as well as a wraparound porch in the rear. The elegant foyer, with its grand staircase, is flanked by the dining room on the left and the study on the right. The island kitchen adjoins the family room and the sunny breakfast nook. The master suite, with an elaborate private bath, is secluded in the back for privacy. Three additional bedrooms—one with a sitting room—share two full baths on the second floor.

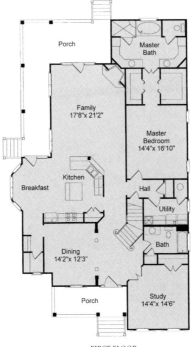

FIRST FLOOR

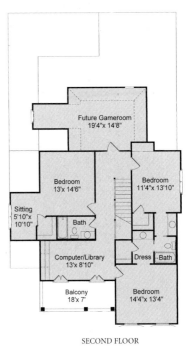

SECOND FLOOR

There's an almost Victorian aspect to this handsome country cottage. The sweeping curved front porch and rear sundeck invite family members and guests to relax and share quiet conversations. A high ceiling in the living room and a sloped ceiling in the adjoining family room simultaneously offer wide-open spaces and intriguing diversity. A curved snack bar easily serves the family room from the kitchen, and a butler's pantry conveniently joins the kitchen and formal dining area. The breakfast nook overlooks the sundeck. The master bedroom has a tray ceiling and enjoys a private bath with an oversize whirlpool tub, His and Hers walk-in closets, and dual vanities. Two more bedrooms, each with walk-in closets, share a luxurious full bath with a tub, shower, and dual sinks on the second floor.

plan# HPK1900100

First Floor: 1,953 sq. ft.
Second Floor: 690 sq. ft.
Total: 2,643 sq. ft.
Bedrooms: 3
Bathrooms: 2½
Width: 64' - 10"
Depth: 52' - 6"
Foundation: Unfinished Walkout Basement

ORDER ONLINE @ EPLANS.COM

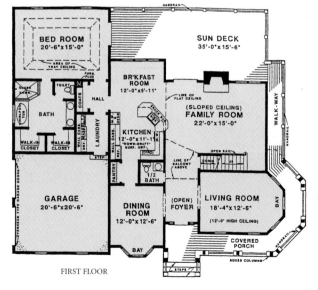

FIRST FLOOR

SECOND FLOOR

plan# HPK1900101

First Floor: 1,009 sq. ft.
Second Floor: 976 sq. ft.
Total: 1,985 sq. ft.
Bedrooms: 3
Bathrooms: 2½
Width: 31' - 2"
Depth: 42' - 0"
Foundation: Unfinished Walkout
Basement, Crawlspace

ORDER ONLINE @ EPLANS.COM

Fine details accentuate the heirlom dollhouse beauty of this narrow-lot Victorian home. Plenty of living space for get-togethers and scaled just right for solitary evenings, the dining room's twin set of French doors can be kept open to expand the space. An eat-in island kitchen makes room for casual meals and offers access to the rear deck. French doors also enhance the family room and provide front-porch access. Two secondary bedrooms share a compartmented bath and enjoy unique windows. The master suite is dressed up with a tray ceiling, French door access to the roomy bath, and a walk-in closet.

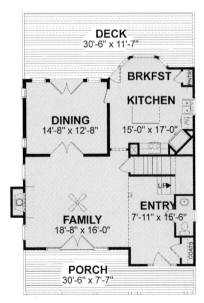

FIRST FLOOR

SECOND FLOOR

A double window highlighted by country shutters is the focal point of this home's facade, which also includes plenty of distinctive stone accents. Inside, the family room features a wall of windows that overlooks the rear covered porch. Lots of counter space, a pantry, and an island cooktop enhance the kitchen; the nearby breakfast nook opens to the porch. Two walk-in closets, a corner tub, and separate shower accent the master bath; the spacious master bedroom, like the great room, is brightened by a wall of windows. Two family bedrooms, one with a walk-in closet, reside upstairs.

plan # HPK1900102

First Floor: 1,510 sq. ft.
Second Floor: 442 sq. ft.
Total: 1,952 sq. ft.
Bedrooms: 3
Bathrooms: 2½
Width: 54' - 7"
Depth: 60' - 3"
Foundation: Slab, Unfinished Basement, Crawlspace

ORDER ONLINE @ EPLANS.COM

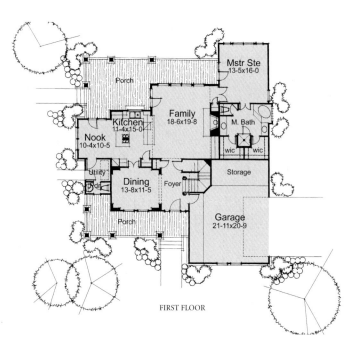

FIRST FLOOR

SECOND FLOOR

plan# HPK1900103

First Floor: 1,356 sq. ft.
Second Floor: 405 sq. ft.
Total: 1,761 sq. ft.
Bedrooms: 3
Bathrooms: 2½
Width: 61' - 5"
Depth: 47' - 8"
Foundation: Crawlspace, Slab,
Unfinished Basement

ORDER ONLINE @ EPLANS.COM

Precise detailing makes this home an inviting and interesting one. Sunburst windows with decorative lintels, two front-facing bay windows, a wraparound porch, and varying rooflines are just some of the elements that accent this home. The foyer leads to the great room, which boasts a large fireplace and French-door access to the master suite—complete with a garden tub and walk-in closet. French doors also lead to the island kitchen and nook with rear-property views. The second floor holds two additional bedrooms, a full bath, and a balcony open to the great room below.

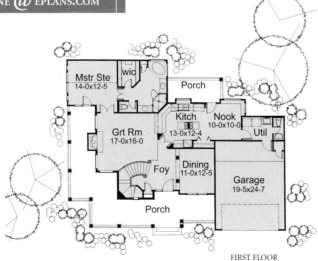

FIRST FLOOR

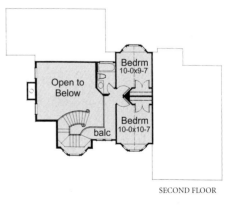

SECOND FLOOR

This gabled two-story farmhouse features a covered front porch flanked by two commanding stone chimneys. Inside, the foyer leads to the living and dining rooms. The living room provides a fireplace and double French doors to the side porch. The kitchen and eating nook are open and easily serve the living area. A private bath pampers the master suite. Two additional bedrooms share a full bath and a balcony space on the second floor.

plan# HPK1900104

First Floor: 1,427 sq. ft.
Second Floor: 545 sq. ft.
Total: 1,972 sq. ft.
Bedrooms: 3
Bathrooms: 2 ½
Width: 59' - 6"
Depth: 40' - 6"
Foundation: Unfinished Basement, Crawlspace, Slab

ORDER ONLINE @ EPLANS.COM

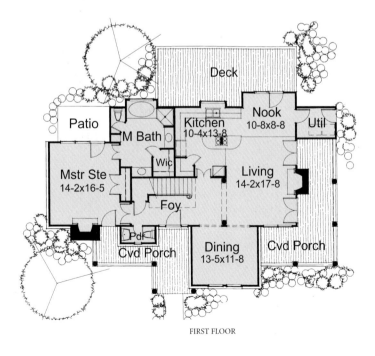

FIRST FLOOR

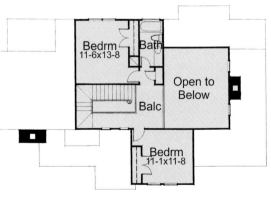

SECOND FLOOR

plan# HPK1900105

First Floor: 1,450 sq. ft.
Second Floor: 448 sq. ft.
Total: 1,898 sq. ft.
Bedrooms: 3
Bathrooms: 2½
Width: 59' - 11"
Depth: 47' - 6"
Foundation: Crawlspace, Slab,
Unfinished Basement

ORDER ONLINE @ EPLANS.COM

This country-style farmhouse features a facade complemented by classic Victorian accents. The wrapping front porch accesses the entry and bayed dining room. The living room and study reside to the front of the plan, and the secluded master bedroom is located at the rear. Master suite amenities include a private bath and roomy walk-in closet. An island kitchen and two-car garage complete the first floor. Upstairs, two additional family bedrooms share a hall bath and balcony overlook to the living room below.

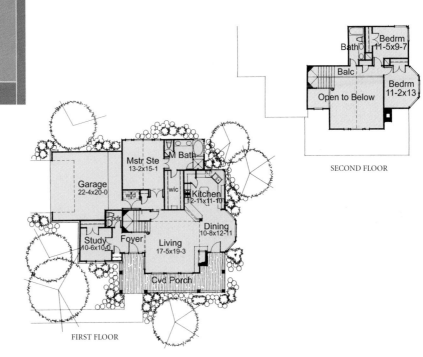

SECOND FLOOR

FIRST FLOOR

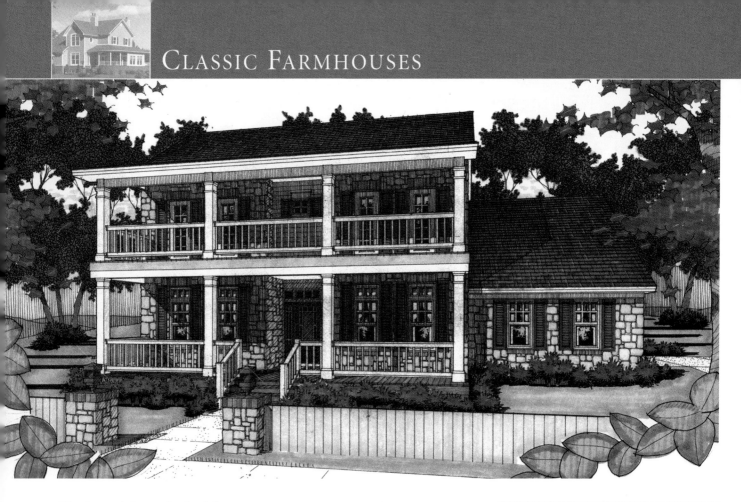

Truly a sight to behold, this home borrows elements from the Colonial styling of the South. Flagstone enhances the facade, and a two-story porch brings out the uniqueness of the design. Enter through the foyer to find a dining room, hearth-warmed great room, and kitchen/nook area; the nook opens to a rear porch. The right side of the plan is home to the master suite with a full bath. Upstairs, two additional bedrooms, a full bath, a covered porch, and a balcony open to the great room below can be found.

plan# HPK1900106

First Floor: 1,320 sq. ft.
Second Floor: 433 sq. ft.
Total: 1,753 sq. ft.
Bedrooms: 3
Bathrooms: 2½
Width: 51' - 11"
Depth: 50' - 0"
Foundation: Crawlspace, Slab,
Unfinished Basement

ORDER ONLINE @ EPLANS.COM

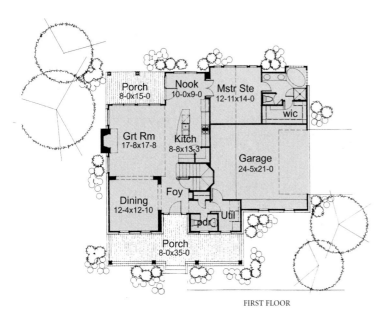

FIRST FLOOR

SECOND FLOOR

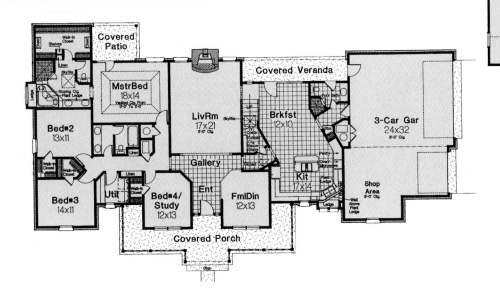

plan# HPK1900107

Square Footage: 2,539
Bonus Space: 636 sq. ft.
Bedrooms: 4
Bathrooms: 3
Width: 98' - 0"
Depth: 53' - 11"
Foundation: Slab, Crawlspace,
Unfinished Basement

ORDER ONLINE @ EPLANS.COM

Rustic corner quoins, a covered front porch, and interesting gables give this home its classic country character. The entry opens to the formal living areas that include a large dining room to the right and a spacious living room warmed by a fireplace straight ahead. A gallery leads the way to the efficient kitchen enhanced with a snack bar and large pantry. Casual meals can be enjoyed overlooking the covered veranda and rear grounds from the connecting breakfast room. The other side of the gallery accesses the luxurious master suite and three secondary bedrooms—all with walk-in closets. The opulent master suite enjoys a private covered patio in the rear of the plan.

Farmhouse fresh with a touch of Victorian style best describes this charming home. A covered front porch wraps around the dining room's bay window and leads the way to the entrance. To the right of the entry is a living room that features a wet bar and a warming fireplace. At the rear of the plan, an L-shaped kitchen is equipped with an island cooktop, making meal preparation a breeze. Casual meals can be enjoyed in a dining area, which merges with the kitchen and accesses the rear patio. A powder room and utility room complete the first floor. Sleeping quarters contained on the second floor include a relaxing master suite with a large walk-in closet, two family bedrooms, and a connecting bath

plan# HPK1900108

First Floor: 1,082 sq. ft.
Second Floor: 838 sq. ft.
Total: 1,920 sq. ft.
Bedrooms: 3
Bathrooms: 2½
Width: 66' - 10"
Depth: 29' - 5"
Foundation: Unfinished Basement, Crawlspace, Slab

ORDER ONLINE @ EPLANS.COM

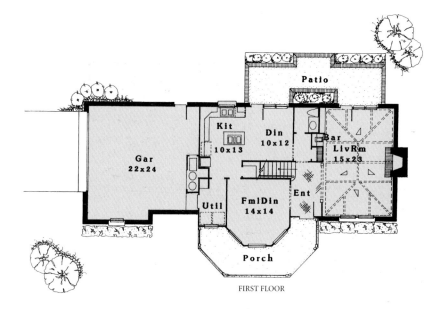

FIRST FLOOR

SECOND FLOOR

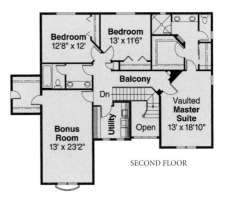

plan# HPK1900109

First Floor: 1,616 sq. ft.

Second Floor: 1,178 sq. ft.

Total: 2,794 sq. ft.

Bonus Space: 409 sq. ft.

Bedrooms: 3

Bathrooms: 3

Width: 64' - 0"

Depth: 55' - 0"

Foundation: Crawlspace

ORDER ONLINE @ EPLANS.COM

It is easy to imagine coming upon this home while meandering in a French village. A decorative iron railing, stone veneer, and multipaned windows add country charm. Everyday family living and special occasions take place in the large, window-bright gathering space on the ground floor. Kitchen, dining and family rooms flow together, linked by a wide arch. A gas fireplace creates a cheerful focal point, and windows fill most of the rear wall. In the dining area, a French door opens onto a partially-covered terrace. Counters wrap around three sides of the kitchen, and more workspace is available on the work island. On the second floor, a balcony overlooks the dramatic, two-story foyer. It also links the master suite on the right with secondary bedrooms, utility room, and a large bonus room on the left.

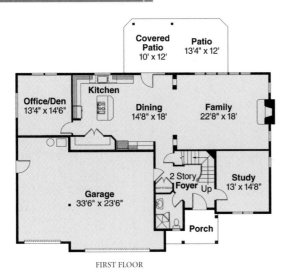

FIRST FLOOR

SECOND FLOOR

Classic keystone arches and lintels run harmonious counterpoint to a rustic background of stone veneer and shake-textured siding. This home can comfortably house a large family. Linked gathering spaces are naturally bright and delightfully spacious. Daylight washes into the two-story foyer through sidelights and a transom. An arch on the right leads into the den, and a wider arch on the left feeds into the dining room. A niche in its rear corner could house a bubbling fountain or a treasured family heirloom. A transverse hallway opens to the vaulted family room on the other side. Windows fill most of the family room's rear wall, offering views of the patio and landscape beyond. Above the gas fireplace is another niche. Just past the stairs, the room flows into a sunny, bayed nook. It's an energizing space to start the day. Counters wrap around three sides of a large kitchen with a generously sized work island. A roomy pantry nestles under the stairs.

plan# HPK1900110

First Floor: 2,480 sq. ft.
Second Floor: 780 sq. ft.
Total: 3,260 sq. ft.
Bonus Space: 981 sq. ft.
Bedrooms: 3
Bathrooms: 2½
Width: 79' - 0"
Depth: 62' - 0"
Foundation: Crawlspace

ORDER ONLINE @ EPLANS.COM

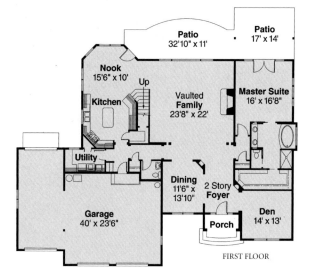

FIRST FLOOR

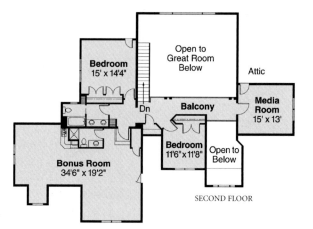

SECOND FLOOR

plan# HPK1900111

First Floor: 1,084 sq. ft.
Second Floor: 461 sq. ft.
Total: 1,545 sq. ft.
Bonus Space: 177 sq. ft.
Bedrooms: 3
Bathrooms: 2½
Width: 38' - 0"
Depth: 61' - 0"
Foundation: Crawlspace

ORDER ONLINE @ EPLANS.COM

A covered porch adds instant curb appeal to any style home, and this traditional favorite is no exception. The first-floor master suite is accessible from the entryway. The open layout makes optimum use of the limited space. The kitchen easily serves the adjoining eating area and family room. A rear patio makes alfresco meals a possibility. Upstairs, two family bedrooms share a full bath. Bonus space on this floor makes a guest room or a game room an option. Extra storage space completes this level.

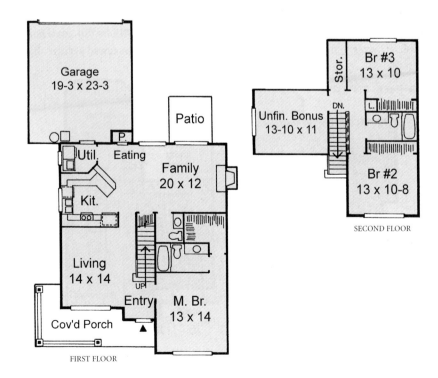

FIRST FLOOR

SECOND FLOOR

Craftsman stylings grace this two-story traditional home, designed for a narrow lot. Shingles and siding present a warm welcome; the front porch opens to the dining room and the gathering room, allowing great entertainment options. The kitchen connects to the living areas with a snack bar and works hard with an island and lots of counter space. The master suite is on this level and delights in a very private bath. Two bedrooms on the upper level have private vanities and a shared bath. Extra storage or bonus space is available for future development.

plan# HPK1900114

First Floor: 1,392 sq. ft.
Second Floor: 708 sq. ft.
Total: 2,100 sq. ft.
Bonus Space: 212 sq. ft.
Bedrooms: 3
Bathrooms: 2½
Width: 32' - 0"
Depth: 55' - 0"
Foundation: Crawlspace

ORDER ONLINE @ EPLANS.COM

FIRST FLOOR

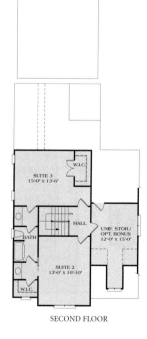

SECOND FLOOR

plan# HPK1900115

First Floor: 680 sq. ft.
Second Floor: 674 sq. ft.
Total: 1,354 sq. ft.
Bedrooms: 3
Bathrooms: 2½
Width: 34' - 5"
Depth: 31' - 3"
Foundation: Slab

ORDER ONLINE @ EPLANS.COM

At first glance you will notice something special about this otherwise traditional Colonial home: past the darling pedimented porch is a brick border running along the entire front facade! Inside, a family room with a corner fireplace awaits. To the right are the eating area and U-shaped, step-saving kitchen with pantry and a laundry room. Upstairs, the master suite has His and Hers closets and a private bath. Two more bedrooms and a full hall bath complete this plan.

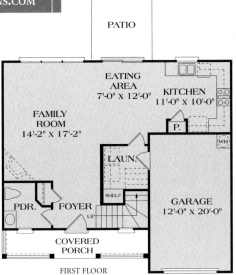

FIRST FLOOR

SECOND FLOOR

This design expands upon the classic double-gabled farmhouse to make room for modern amenities like a three-car garage and a first-floor master suite. Traditional symmetry is maintained in the front rooms that flank the foyer; in this case, a formal dining room and a flexible space that could serve as a parlor, study, or even a bedroom. An arched opening gives way to a more contemporary open floor plan that includes a spacious gathering room with a three-way fireplace and a kitchen snack bar. Choose from an open or a screened porch for outdoor meals. Upstairs, two generously sized bedrooms share a dual-sink bath, and a large game room over the garage provides kids with living space of their own.

ptan# HPK1900116

First Floor: 1,467 sq. ft.
Second Floor: 513 sq. ft.
Total: 1,980 sq. ft.
Bedrooms: 3
Bathrooms: 2½
Width: 68' - 0"
Depth: 53' - 0"

ORDER ONLINE @ EPLANS.COM

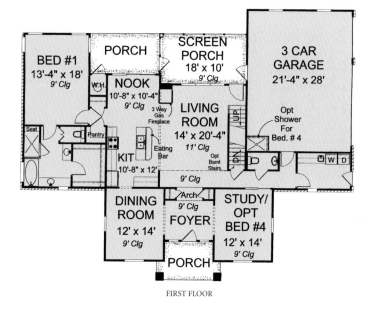

FIRST FLOOR

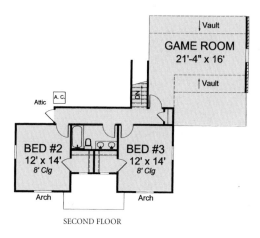

SECOND FLOOR

plan# HPK1900117

First Floor: 1,383 sq. ft.

Second Floor: 703 sq. ft.

Total: 2,086 sq. ft.

Bonus Space: 342 sq. ft.

Bedrooms: 4

Bathrooms: 3½

Width: 49' - 0"

Depth: 50' - 0"

ORDER ONLINE @ EPLANS.COM

This enchanting farmhouse looks great in the country, on the waterfront, or on your street! Inside, the foyer is accented by a barrel arch and opens on the right to a formal dining room. An 11-foot ceiling in the living room expands the space, as a warming fireplace makes it feel cozy. The step-saving kitchen easily serves the bayed breakfast nook. In the sumptuous master suite, a sitting area is bathed in natural light, and the walk-in closet is equipped with a built-in dresser. The luxurious bath features dual vanities and a spa tub. Three upstairs bedrooms, one with a private bath, access optional future space, designed to meet your family's needs.

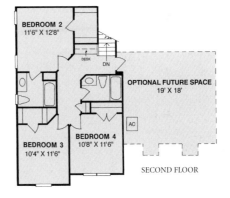

SECOND FLOOR

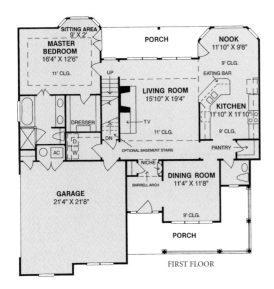

FIRST FLOOR

Make the most of square footage by eliminating superfluous rooms and enlarging the essential ones. High ceilings and tall windows across the long back wall of the home also lend their influence to the sense of spaciousness. Clutter-free order will reign, thanks to plenty of storage, including walk-in pantry and closets, a utility room, and a large area off the garage. But the home's charm comes from more than practical considerations. It also offers a country-style porch in front and a private porch off the homeowner's suite. The orderly master bath is guaranteed to become a favorite place to destress. And upstairs, kids can enjoy a world of their own, with two generously sized bedrooms, a shared bath, and a room for games or studying. If that's not enough, a more secluded space above the garage can be finished off as needed.

plan# HPK1900118

First Floor: 1,850 sq. ft.
Second Floor: 854 sq. ft.
Total: 2,704 sq. ft.
Bonus Space: 315 sq. ft.
Bedrooms: 3
Bathrooms: 2½
Width: 84' - 5"
Depth: 45' - 10"
Foundation: Crawlspace, Slab, Unfinished Basement

ORDER ONLINE @ EPLANS.COM

FIRST FLOOR

SECOND FLOOR

plan # HPK1900119

First Floor: 1,849 sq. ft.
Second Floor: 855 sq. ft.
Total: 2,704 sq. ft.
Bedrooms: 4
Bathrooms: 3½
Width: 69' - 0"
Depth: 55' - 8"

ORDER ONLINE @ EPLANS.COM

The Craftsman influence lightly touches this gabled farmhouse, accenting the facade with coupled columns and artful windows. Inside, however, the plan is all about the 21st-century family. The three-car garage opens into a vestibule containing benches, cabinets, and a row of lockers. The laundry room is conveniently located here as well. The spacious kitchen features a walk-in pantry and an angled island where the family can assemble for informal chatter as dinner is prepared. A window-bright eating area opens to the vaulted great room, where a corner fireplace facilitates cozy gatherings. A tray-ceilinged room off the foyer may be furnished as a dining room or a den. The first-floor master suite contains all the amenities that modern homeowners desire: dual vanities, oversized shower, and a huge walk-in closet. Upstairs, two bedrooms share a compartmented bath, and a third bedroom with private bath makes excellent quarters for guests or an older child.

OPTIONAL LAYOUT

FIRST FLOOR

SECOND FLOOR

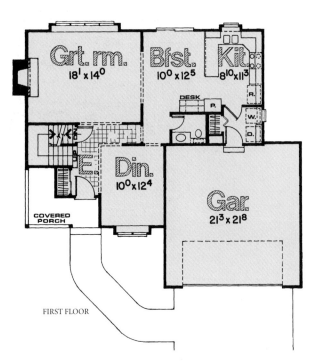

This modestly sized home provides a quaint covered front porch that opens to a two-story foyer. The formal dining room features a boxed window that can be seen from the entry. A fireplace in the great room adds warmth and coziness to the attached breakfast room and the well-planned kitchen. A powder room is nearby for guests. Three bedrooms occupy the second floor; one of these includes an arched window under a vaulted ceiling. The deluxe master suite provides a large walk-in closet and a dressing area with a double vanity and a whirlpool tub.

plan# HPK1900120

First Floor: 891 sq. ft.
Second Floor: 759 sq. ft.
Total: 1,650 sq. ft.
Bedrooms: 3
Bathrooms: 2½
Width: 44' - 0"
Depth: 40' - 0"

ORDER ONLINE @ EPLANS.COM

FIRST FLOOR

SECOND FLOOR

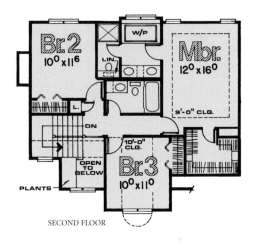

plan# HPK1900121

First Floor: 1,082 sq. ft.
Second Floor: 1,021 sq. ft.
Total: 2,103 sq. ft.
Bedrooms: 4
Bathrooms: 2½
Width: 50' - 0"
Depth: 40' - 0"

ORDER ONLINE @ EPLANS.COM

A covered porch invites you into this country-style home. Handsome book-cases frame the fireplace in the spacious family room. Double doors off the entry provide the family room with added privacy. The kitchen features an island, a lazy Susan, and easy access to a laundry room. The master bedroom features a boxed ceiling and separate entries to a walk-in closet and a pampering bath. The upstairs hall bath is compartmented, allowing maximum usage for today's busy family.

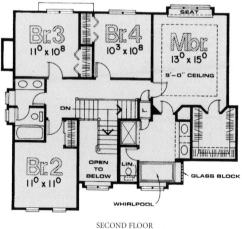

SECOND FLOOR

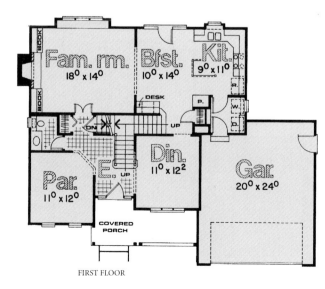

FIRST FLOOR

What a combination

What a combination—a charming turn-of-the-century exterior with a contemporary interior! A wraparound railed porch and rear deck expand the living space to outdoor entertaining. Vaulted ceilings throughout the great room and dining room add spaciousness; a fireplace warms the area. An open kitchen plan includes a preparation island, breakfast bar, and window over the sink. The master suite is on the first floor for privacy and convenience. It boasts a roomy walk-in closet and private bath with a garden whirlpool tub, separate shower, and dual vanities. Two vaulted family bedrooms on the second floor share a full bath. Note the loft area and extra storage space.

plan# HPK1900122

First Floor: 1,050 sq. ft.
Second Floor: 533 sq. ft.
Total: 1,583 sq. ft.
Bedrooms: 3
Bathrooms: 2
Width: 42' - 0"
Depth: 38' - 0"
Foundation: Crawlspace, Unfinished Basement

ORDER ONLINE @ EPLANS.COM

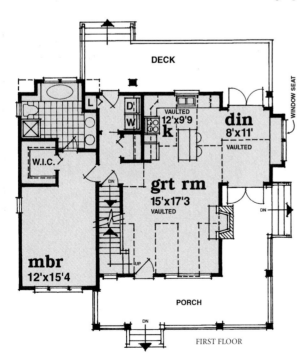

FIRST FLOOR

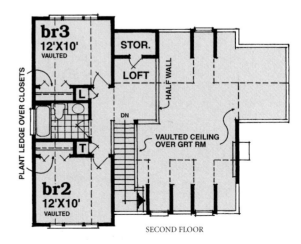

SECOND FLOOR

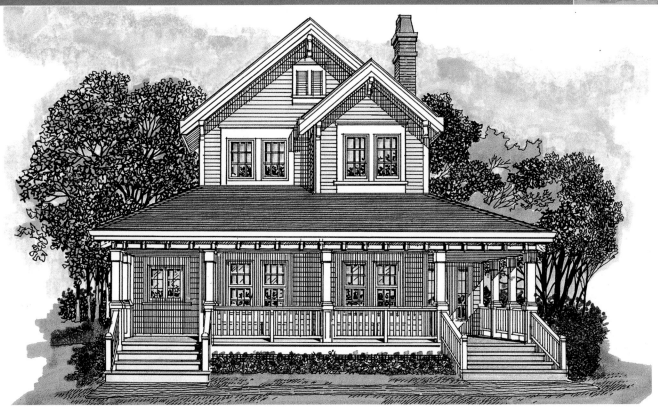

plan# HPK1900123

First Floor: 995 sq. ft.
Second Floor: 484 sq. ft.
Total: 1,479 sq. ft.
Bedrooms: 3
Bathrooms: 2½
Width: 38' - 0"
Depth: 44' - 0"
Foundation: Crawlspace, Unfinished Basement

ORDER ONLINE @ EPLANS.COM

What an appealing plan! Its rustic character is defined by cedar lattice, covered columned porches, exposed rafters, and multipane, double-hung windows. The great room/dining room combination is reached through double doors off the veranda and features a fireplace towering two stories to the lofty ceiling. A U-shaped kitchen contains an angled snack counter that serves this area and loads of space for a breakfast table—or use the handy side porch for alfresco dining. To the rear resides the master bedroom with a full bath and double doors to the veranda. An additional half-bath sits just beyond the laundry room. Upstairs, two family bedrooms and a full bath finish the plan.

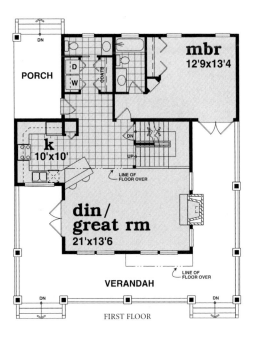

FIRST FLOOR

SECOND FLOOR

Covered porches at the front and rear make this a very comfortable farmhouse. Double doors open to the foyer, flanked by the formal dining room and sunken living room. A butler's pantry, complete with a wet bar, separates the dining room and L-shaped island kitchen. A sunny breakfast room adjoins the kitchen on one side and the family room with a fireplace on the other. Double doors open to the rear porch. The master suite on the second level offers a walk-in closet and full bath with a corner whirlpool tub, separate shower, and double vanity. Three family bedrooms share a full bath that includes a dressing room with a vanity. The two-car garage connects to the main house via a service area/laundry room.

plan # HPK1900124

First Floor: 1,261 sq. ft.
Second Floor: 1,185 sq. ft.
Total: 2,446 sq. ft.
Bedrooms: 4
Bathrooms: 2½
Width: 60' - 0"
Depth: 44' - 0"
Foundation: Unfinished Basement, Crawlspace

ORDER ONLINE @ EPLANS.COM

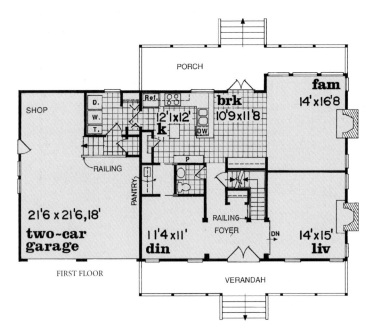

FIRST FLOOR

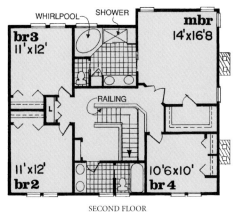

SECOND FLOOR

© 1996 Donald A. Gardner Architects, Inc

plan# HPK1900125

First Floor: 875 sq. ft.
Second Floor: 814 sq. ft.
Total: 1,689 sq. ft.
Bedrooms: 3
Bathrooms: 2½
Width: 37' - 0"
Depth: 51' - 0"

ORDER ONLINE @ EPLANS.COM

Double gables and a covered porch give this narrow-lot home a storybook beginning. Inside, a thoughtfully arranged floor plan provides efficiency that translates into happily ever after for the entire family. A rear deck expands outdoor living space from the great room, which is open to a center island kitchen. Formal dining is enhanced by a bay window and a columned entry that graces this room. The second floor contains a relaxing master suite that features a private bath filled with amenities and two family bedrooms that share a full bath.

FIRST FLOOR

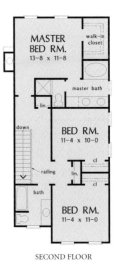

SECOND FLOOR

© 2000 Donald A. Gardner, Inc.

Here's a country home with plenty of open interior space. Just off the foyer, a powder room and coat closet are thoughtfully placed to accommodate guests. A fireplace and built-ins highlight the great room. A formal dining room adjoins the kitchen and breakfast area, which features a triple window. Wrapping counter space in the kitchen provides enough food-preparation space for two cooks. The master suite includes a walk-in closet, well-appointed bath, and additional linen storage. Upstairs, two family bedrooms share a hall bath and access to a spacious bonus room.

plan ⏴#⏵ HPK1900126

First Floor: 1,412 sq. ft.
Second Floor: 506 sq. ft.
Total: 1,918 sq. ft.
Bonus Space: 320 sq. ft.
Bedrooms: 3
Bathrooms: 2½
Width: 49' - 8"
Depth: 52' - 0"

ORDER ONLINE @ EPLANS.COM

FIRST FLOOR

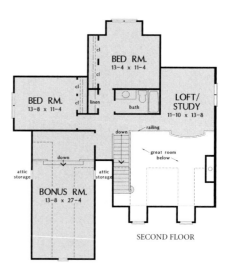

SECOND FLOOR

ORDER BLUEPRINTS 24 HOURS, 7 DAYS A WEEK, AT 1-800-521-6797

© 1998 Donald A. Gardner Architects, Inc.

plan# HPK1900127

First Floor: 1,614 sq. ft.
Second Floor: 892 sq. ft.
Total: 2,506 sq. ft.
Bonus Space: 341 sq. ft.
Bedrooms: 4
Bathrooms: 2½
Width: 71' - 10"
Depth: 50' - 0"

ORDER ONLINE @ EPLANS.COM

At the front of this farmhouse design, the master suite includes a sitting bay, two walk-in closets, a door to the front porch, and a compartmented bath with a double-bowl vanity. The formal dining room in the second bay also features a door to the front porch. Access the rear porch from the great room, which opens to the breakfast room under the balcony. On the second floor, three family bedrooms share a bath that has a double-bowl vanity. One of the family bedrooms offers a walk-in closet. A bonus room over the garage can be used as a study or game room.

SECOND FLOOR

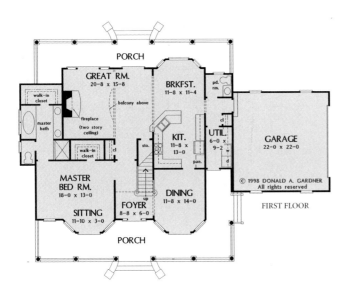

FIRST FLOOR

© 1996 Donald A. Gardner Architects, Inc.

Eye-catching twin chimneys dominate the exterior of this grand design, but on closer approach you will delight in the covered porch with decorated pediment and the tall windows across the front of the house. A long hallway separates the family room, with a fireplace, from the rest of the house. A large U-shaped kitchen features an island work center and direct access to the sunny breakfast room and the formal dining room. A study/living room (with an optional second fireplace) completes the first floor. Upstairs, you'll find a well-appointed master suite, two family bedrooms, and a bonus room over the garage.

plan# HPK1900128

First Floor: 1,428 sq. ft.
Second Floor: 1,067 sq. ft.
Total: 2,495 sq. ft.
Bonus Space: 342 sq. ft.
Bedrooms: 3
Bathrooms: 2½
Width: 74' - 0"
Depth: 64' - 8"

ORDER ONLINE @ EPLANS.COM

© 1996 Donald A. Gardner Architects, Inc.

FIRST FLOOR

SECOND FLOOR

plan# HPK1900129

First Floor: 1,086 sq. ft.
Second Floor: 554 sq. ft.
Total: 1,640 sq. ft.
Bedrooms: 3
Bathrooms: 2
Width: 52' - 0"
Depth: 43' - 0"
Foundation: Crawlspace

ORDER ONLINE @ EPLANS.COM

A touch of tradition provides a versatile exterior for this delight-fully comfortable farmhouse. A wraparound porch, a welcoming entrance, and a thoughtful floor plan make this house a pleasure to come home to. The foyer, featuring a built-in seat with shoe storage, opens onto a large great room. A fireplace framed by unique windows warms this area. The adjacent nook and efficient U-shaped kitchen combine with the great room to create a spacious area for gatherings. Split from family bedrooms for privacy, the relaxing master suite is enhanced by a pampering bath, large walk-in closet, and porch access. Skylights brighten the second-floor bridge that connects two family bedrooms to a full bath.

SECOND FLOOR

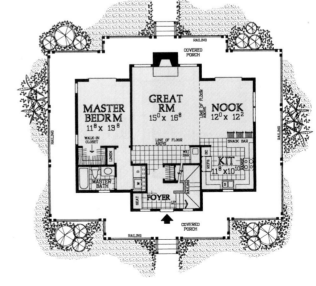

FIRST FLOOR

A Palladian window, fish-scale shingles, and turret-style bays set off this country-style Victorian exterior. Muntin windows and a quintessential wraparound porch dress up an understated theme and introduce an unrestrained floor plan with plenty of bays and niches. An impressive tiled entry opens to the formal rooms that nestle to the left side of the plan and enjoy natural light from an abundance of windows. The turret houses a secluded study on the first floor and provides a sunny bay window for a family bedroom upstairs. The second-floor master suite boasts its own fireplace, a dressing area with a walk-in closet, and a lavish bath with a garden tub and twin vanities. The two-car garage offers space for a workshop or extra storage and leads to a service entrance to the walk-through utility room

plan# HPK1900132

First Floor: 1,186 sq. ft.
Second Floor: 988 sq. ft.
Total: 2,174 sq. ft.
Bedrooms: 4
Bathrooms: 2½
Width: 72' - 0"
Depth: 50' - 10"
Foundation: Unfinished Basement

ORDER ONLINE @ EPLANS.COM

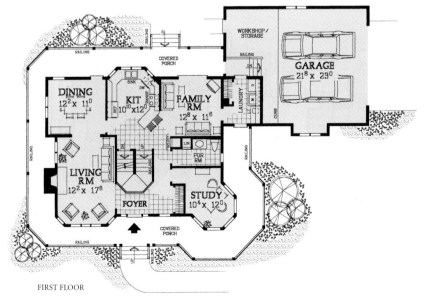

FIRST FLOOR

SECOND FLOOR

© William E. Poole Designs, Inc.

plan # HPK1900133

First Floor: 1,913 sq. ft.
Second Floor: 997 sq. ft.
Total: 2,910 sq. ft.
Bonus Space: 377 sq. ft.
Bedrooms: 4
Bathrooms: 3½
Width: 63' - 0"
Depth: 59' - 4"
Foundation: Crawlspace, Unfinished Basement

ORDER ONLINE @ EPLANS.COM

This enchanting farmhouse brings the past to life with plenty of modern amenities. An open-flow kitchen/breakfast area and family room combination is the heart of the home, opening up to the screened porch and enjoying the warmth of a fireplace. For more formal occasions, the foyer is flanked by a living room on the left and a dining room on the right. An elegant master bedroom, complete with a super-sized walk-in closet, is tucked away quietly behind the garage. Three more bedrooms reside upstairs, along with two full baths and a future recreation room.

FIRST FLOOR

SECOND FLOOR

Note the clean lines and attractive front porch of this symmetrical design. Inside, the two-story foyer is flanked by a formal living room and a more casual great room. Two sun rooms echo each other at opposite ends of the home. The U-shaped kitchen offers a snack bar into the great room and has access to the rear deck. If entertaining is your forte, the formal dining room flows into the formal living room, perfect for after-dinner conversation. Upstairs, a lavish master bedroom features a walk-in closet, private fireplace, and sumptuous private bath. Two large secondary bedrooms and a hall bath complete this level.

plan# HPK1900134

First Floor: 1,008 sq. ft.
Second Floor: 917 sq. ft.
Total: 1,925 sq. ft.
Bedrooms: 3
Bathrooms: 2½
Width: 56' - 0"
Depth: 36' - 0"
Foundation: Crawlspace, Unfinished Basement

ORDER ONLINE @ EPLANS.COM

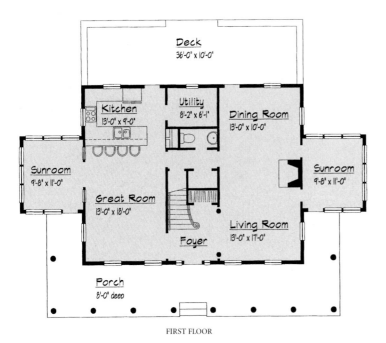

Deck
36'-0" x 10'-0"

Kitchen
13'-0" x 9'-0"

Utility
8'-2" x 6'-1"

Dining Room
13'-0" x 10'-0"

Sunroom
9'-8" x 11'-0"

Sunroom
9'-8" x 11'-0"

Great Room
13'-0" x 18'-0"

Foyer

Living Room
13'-0" x 17'-0"

Porch
8'-0" deep

FIRST FLOOR

Master Bedroom
13'-0" x 17'-6"

Balcony

open to Foyer below

Bedroom
13'-0" x 12'-6"

Bedroom
13'-0" x 11'-10"

SECOND FLOOR

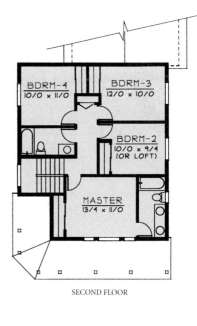

plan # HPK1900135

First Floor: 858 sq. ft.
Second Floor: 791 sq. ft.
Total: 1,649 sq. ft.
Bedrooms: 4
Bathrooms: 2½
Width: 30' - 0"
Depth: 52' - 0"
Foundation: Crawlspace

ORDER ONLINE @ EPLANS.COM

Traditional wood shingles and horizontal siding enhance and characterize the exterior of this country craftsman cottage. With appealing exterior bungalow styling, this home is perfect for a narrow lot. A quaint covered front porch welcomes you inside. Downstairs, the floor plan is very open and spacious. The island kitchen features a useful eating bar. The plan boasts four family bedrooms, two full baths, and one half-bath. The rear two-car garage features a side entry.

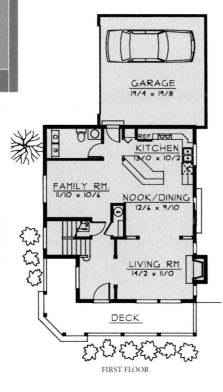

FIRST FLOOR

SECOND FLOOR

Traditional wood siding gives a look of down-home comfort to this charming two-story home. A brief foyer opens to the family room that is highlighted with a fireplace and pass-through to the kitchen. The efficient kitchen has wrapping counters, a breakfast nook, laundry center, and easy service to the dining room. Upstairs, the master suite has elegant ceiling detail, a vaulted bath, and roomy walk-in closet. Two family bedrooms share a hall bath.

plan# HPK1900136

First Floor: 719 sq. ft.
Second Floor: 717 sq. ft.
Total: 1,436 sq. ft.
Bonus Space: 290 sq. ft.
Bedrooms: 3
Bathrooms: 2½
Width: 45' - 10"
Depth: 35' - 6"
Foundation: Crawlspace, Slab, Unfinished Walkout Basement

ORDER ONLINE @ EPLANS.COM

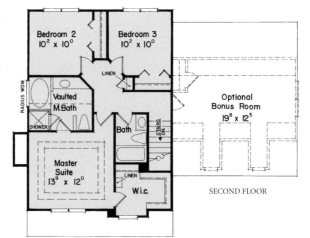

FIRST FLOOR

SECOND FLOOR

plan# HPK1900137

First Floor: 1,725 sq. ft.
Second Floor: 992 sq. ft.
Total: 2,717 sq. ft.
Bonus Space: 351 sq. ft.
Bedrooms: 3
Bathrooms: 2½
Width: 46' - 0"
Depth: 85' - 0"
Foundation: Slab, Crawlspace

ORDER ONLINE @ EPLANS.COM

A covered front porch provides three means of entrance—the front door into the foyer, a side door near the pantry, or French doors into the dining room. The island kitchen offers a serving bar to the coffer-ceilinged, hearth-warmed family room and access to the breakfast area, with yet another door leading outside. The master suite envelops the left side of the plan. The bath, with two sinks, compartmented toilet, and a separate tub and shower, is to be admired. Two bedrooms upstairs are convenient to a spacious recreation room—so let the kids play!

Bonus Room
21⁶ x 19⁵

FIRST FLOOR

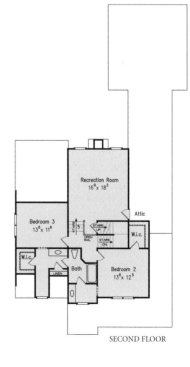

SECOND FLOOR

A covered porch makes for great socializing and curb appeal, beneath an exterior abounding with fenestration. An elongated foyer is flanked by a formal dining room, which opens to the right, lined with decorative columns. A split staircase follows, leading to the generous, vaulted family room. A sunny and casual breakfast room and kitchen lie to the left, with views of and access to the rear property afforded from the nook. The master suite, tucked in the rear left corner of the plan, is vaulted, and will pamper the female head of household with an enormous walk-in closet.

plan# HPK1900138

First Floor: 1,472 sq. ft.
Second Floor: 724 sq. ft.
Total: 2,196 sq. ft.
Bonus Space: 300 sq. ft.
Bedrooms: 4
Bathrooms: 2½
Width: 52' - 4"
Depth: 52' - 0"
Foundation: Crawlspace, Unfinished Walkout Basement, Slab

ORDER ONLINE @ EPLANS.COM

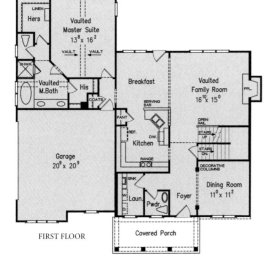

FIRST FLOOR

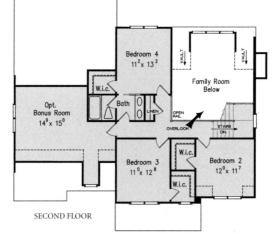

SECOND FLOOR

plan# HPK1900139

First Floor: 1,407 sq. ft.
Second Floor: 472 sq. ft.
Total: 1,879 sq. ft.
Bonus Space: 321 sq. ft.
Bedrooms: 3
Bathrooms: 2½
Width: 48' - 0"
Depth: 53' - 10"
Foundation: Crawlspace, Unfinished
Walkout Basement

ORDER ONLINE @ EPLANS.COM

This captivating three-bedroom home combines the rustic, earthy feel of cut stone with the crisp look of siding to create a design that will be the hallmark of your neighborhood. From the impressive two-story foyer, the vaulted family room lies straight ahead. The extended-hearth fireplace can be viewed from the kitchen via a serving bar that accesses the breakfast nook. The vaulted dining room is an elegant space for formal occasions. The first-floor master suite includes a pampering bath and dual walk-in closets, one with linen storage. Upstairs, a short hall and family-room overlook separate the bedrooms. Bonus space can serve as a home office, playroom . . . anything your family desires.

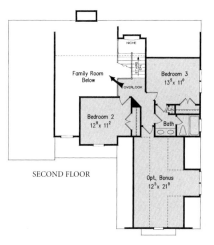

SECOND FLOOR

FIRST FLOOR

This striking design is reminiscent of the grand homes of the past century. Its wood siding and covered porch are complemented by shuttered windows and a glass-paneled entry. Historic design is updated in the floor plan to include a vaulted living room, a two-story family room, and a den that doubles as a guest suite on the first floor. Second-floor bedrooms feature a master suite with tray ceiling and vaulted bath. An optional loft on the second floor may be finished as a study area.

plan# HPK1900140

First Floor: 1,415 sq. ft.
Second Floor: 1,015 sq. ft.
Total: 2,430 sq. ft.
Bonus Space: 169 sq. ft.
Bedrooms: 4
Bathrooms: 3½
Width: 54' - 0"
Depth: 43' - 4"
Foundation: Unfinished Walkout Basement, Crawlspace

ORDER ONLINE @ EPLANS.COM

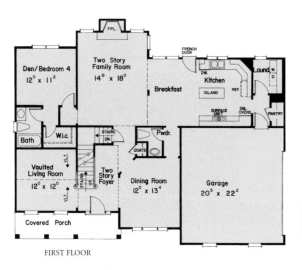

FIRST FLOOR

SECOND FLOOR

plan# HPK1900141

First Floor: 1,223 sq. ft.
Second Floor: 1,163 sq. ft.
Total: 2,386 sq. ft.
Bonus Space: 204 sq. ft.
Bedrooms: 4
Bathrooms: 2½
Width: 50' - 0"
Depth: 48' - 0"
Foundation: Crawlspace, Unfinished
Walkout Basement

ORDER ONLINE @ EPLANS.COM

Classic capstones and arched windows complement rectangular shutters and pillars on this traditional facade. The family room offsets a formal dining room and shares a see-through fireplace with the keeping room. The gourmet kitchen boasts a food-preparation island with a serving bar, a generous pantry, and French-door access to the rear property. Upstairs, a sensational master suite—with a tray ceiling and a vaulted bath with a plant shelf, whirlpool spa, and walk-in closet—opens from a gallery hall with a balcony overlook. Bonus space offers the possibility of an adjoining sitting room. Three additional bedrooms share a full bath.

SECOND FLOOR

FIRST FLOOR

Only a sloping pediment above double front windows adorns this simple, country-style house, where a side-entry garage looks like a rambling addition. The wide porch signals a welcome that continues throughout the house. A front study doubles as a guest room with an adjacent full bath. A large dining room is ideal for entertaining and a sun-filled breakfast room off a spacious kitchen provides comfortable space for casual family meals. The open, contemporary interior plan flows from a stair hall at the heart of the house. On the private second floor, the master bedroom includes a luxurious bath; two other bedrooms share a bath that includes dual vanities. An extra room over the kitchen makes a perfect children's play area.

plan # HPK1900142

First Floor: 1,634 sq. ft.
Second Floor: 1,598 sq. ft.
Total: 3,232 sq. ft.
Bonus Space: 273 sq. ft.
Bedrooms: 3
Bathrooms: 3
Width: 62' - 0"
Depth: 54' - 9"
Foundation: Finished Walkout Basement

ORDER ONLINE @ EPLANS.COM

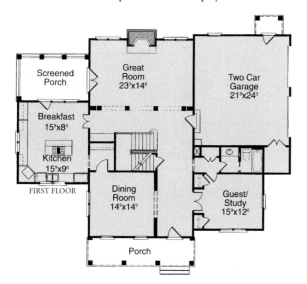

FIRST FLOOR

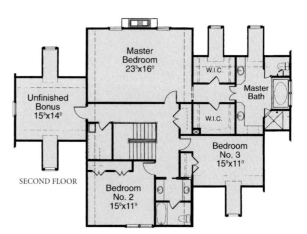

SECOND FLOOR

plan# HPK1900143

First Floor: 1,840 sq. ft.
Second Floor: 950 sq. ft.
Total: 2,790 sq. ft.
Bedrooms: 4
Bathrooms: 3½
Width: 58' - 6"
Depth: 62' - 0"
Foundation: Finished Walkout
Basement

ORDER ONLINE @ EPLANS.COM

The appearance of this Early American home brings the past to mind with its wraparound porch, wood siding, and flower-box detailing. Inside, columns frame the great room and the dining room. Left of the foyer lies the living room with a warming fireplace. The angular kitchen joins a sunny breakfast nook. The master bedroom has a spacious private bath and a walk-in closet. Stairs to the second level lead from the breakfast area to an open landing overlooking the great room. Three family bedrooms—two with walk-in closets and all three with private access to a bath—complete this level.

SECOND FLOOR

FIRST FLOOR

Quaint keystones and shutters offer charming accents to the stucco-and-stone exterior of this stately English Country home. The two-story foyer opens through decorative columns to the formal living room, which offers a wet bar. The nearby media room shares a through-fireplace with the two-story great room, which has double doors that lead to the rear deck. A bumped-out bay holds a breakfast area that shares its light with an expansive cooktop-island kitchen. This area opens to the formal dining room through a convenient butler's pantry. One wing of the second floor is dedicated to the rambling master suite, which boasts unusual amenities with angled walls, a tray ceiling, and a bumped-out bay with a sitting area in the bedroom.

plan# HPK1900144

First Floor: 1,475 sq. ft.
Second Floor: 1,460 sq. ft.
Total: 2,935 sq. ft.
Bedrooms: 4
Bathrooms: 3½
Width: 57' - 6"
Depth: 46' - 6"
Foundation: Finished Walkout Basement

ORDER ONLINE @ EPLANS.COM

FIRST FLOOR

SECOND FLOOR

ORDER BLUEPRINTS 24 HOURS, 7 DAYS A WEEK, AT 1-800-521-6797

COUNTRY ESTATES

PHOTO BY BOB GREENSPAN

Country estates take the classic farmhouse design to the next level of luxury. They combine the quaint details of country style with the demands of today's desire for a home to serve not just as a living place but as a relaxing retreat.

Estate homes were historically built by wealthy landowners on plantations or premium country acreage. With a larger budget than your average farmer and the introduction of cross-country transportation and shipping, these homeowners had the luxury of incorporating a number of styles and materials into their designs. Victorian homes with artful embellishments were most popular in the late 1800s, when the industrial revolution was booming. Queen Anne designs and European-influenced revivals were symbols of wealth during this time, when industry thrived in post-Civil War America and building materials were more affordably produced.

Today, country estates cover a wide range of styles, from sprawling Craftsman bungalows to towering Victorian mansions to broad southern plantations. With so much more square footage, the possibilities for bonus living space are endless. The shallow pitch of a Craftsman home suggests a warm climate where little snow will weigh on the roof. This design may reduce finished attic space, but the low design and temperate weather are a perfect combination for additional informal great rooms and outdoor living areas. Victorian turrets invite cozy reading nooks and home offices with 180 degree views. Breadth, height, and signature porches provide room for guest suites and gathering places for friends and family in the plantations and larger classic farmhouses. While maintaining their historical character, these homes incorporate the most modern of amenities for every lifestyle: spacious His and Hers walk-in closets, pampering first-floor master suites, additional suites for guests and in-laws, wet bars for entertaining, plus family-oriented media and rec rooms, just to name a few.

Above: Fine details evoke the design's sense of history. See more of this home on page 157.

The lacy veranda that embraces the exterior of this Queen Anne home offers outdoor living space under its shady recesses. Inside, the great room features a fireplace, built-in shelves, and a wet bar. The kitchen boasts a walk-in pantry, an island countertop, a breakfast nook with a bayed window, and access to the keeping room and the rear covered porch. The second floor contains three family bedrooms and the master suite. The elegant master suite features a sitting area located within a turret, a spacious walk-in closet, an enormous bath with a step-up tub and dual vanities, and access to its own private exercise room. This home is designed with a two-car garage.

plan# HPK1900145

First Floor: 2,506 sq. ft.
Second Floor: 2,315 sq. ft.
Total: 4,821 sq. ft.
Bedrooms: 5
Bathrooms: 4
Width: 60' - 0"
Depth: 97' - 0"
Foundation: Crawlspace

ORDER ONLINE @ EPLANS.COM

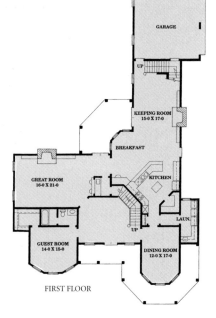

FIRST FLOOR

SECOND FLOOR

plan # HPK1900146

First Floor: 1,600 sq. ft.
Second Floor: 790 sq. ft.
Total: 2,390 sq. ft.
Bedrooms: 4
Bathrooms: 3½
Width: 45' - 0"
Depth: 54' - 0"
Foundation: Crawlspace

ORDER ONLINE @ EPLANS.COM

Queen Anne houses, with their projecting bays, towers, and wraparound porches, were the apex of the Victorian era. This up-to-date rendition of the beloved style captures a floor plan that is as dramatic on the inside as it is on the outside. The front-facing pediment ornamented with typical gable detailing highlights the front doorway and provides additional welcome to this enchanted abode. The angles and bays that occur in every first-floor room add visual excitement to formal and informal living and dining areas. A well-lit breakfast bay with its soaring ceiling is a spectacular addition to this classic plan. The first-floor master suite features two walk-in closets. Three upstairs bedrooms also have spacious walk-in closets.

FIRST FLOOR

SECOND FLOOR

PHOTO BY: RUSSELL KINGMAN/HDS

The turret and the circular covered porch of this Victorian home make a great impression. The foyer carries you past a library and dining room to the hearth-warmed family room. A spacious kitchen with an island acts as a passageway to the nook and dining area. The master bedroom is located on the first floor and offers its own French doors to the rear covered porch. The master bath is designed to cater to both His and Her needs with two walk-in closets, separate vanities, a garden tub, and separate shower. The second-floor balcony looks to the family room below.

plan# HPK1900147

First Floor: 2,041 sq. ft.
Second Floor: 1,098 sq. ft.
Total: 3,139 sq. ft.
Bonus Space: 385 sq. ft.
Bedrooms: 4
Bathrooms: 3½
Width: 76' - 6"
Depth: 62' - 2"
Foundation: Slab

ORDER ONLINE @ EPLANS.COM

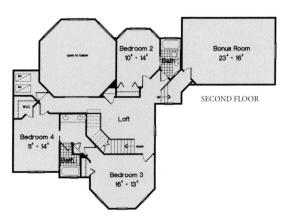

FIRST FLOOR

SECOND FLOOR

plan# HPK1900148

First Floor: 4,383 sq. ft.

Second Floor: 1,557 sq. ft.

Total: 5,940 sq. ft.

Bedrooms: 4

Bathrooms: 5½

Width: 148' - 8"

Depth: 120' - 5"

Foundation: Unfinished Basement

ORDER ONLINE @ EPLANS.COM

Victorian-inspired, this estate home is rife with details and grand appointments. The central foyer opens from double doors on the wrapping veranda and leads to a parlor on the right and a study on the left. The parlor shares a through-fireplace with the formal dining room. A keeping room at the back is open to the island kitchen. A service hall leads to the three-car garage, which has a 788-square-foot apartment above. A media room and the master suite round out the first level. The second level holds three bedrooms with three private baths. A terrace opens from double doors on the west gallery.

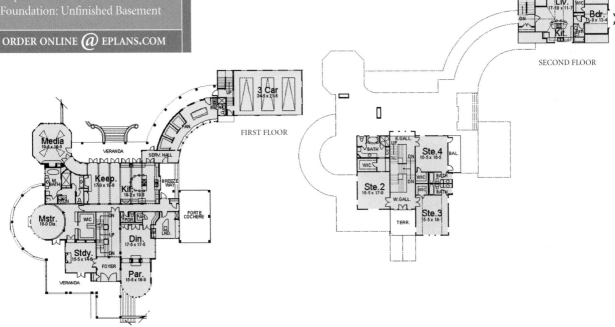

SECOND FLOOR

FIRST FLOOR

A wraparound covered porch adds plenty of outdoor space to this already impressive home. Built-in cabinets flank the fireplace in the grand room; a fireplace also warms the hearth room. The gourmet kitchen includes an island counter, large walk-in pantry, and serving bar. A secluded home office, with a separate entrance nearby, provides a quiet work place. A front parlor provides even more room for entertaining or relaxing. The master suite dominates the second floor, offering a spacious sitting area with an elegant tray ceiling, a dressing area, and a luxurious bath with two walk-in closets, double vanities, and a raised garden tub. The second floor is also home to an enormous exercise room and three additional bedrooms.

plan# HPK1900149

First Floor: 2,732 sq. ft.
Second Floor: 2,734 sq. ft.
Total: 5,466 sq. ft.
Bedrooms: 5
Bathrooms: 5½ + ½
Width: 85' - 0"
Depth: 85' - 6"
Foundation: Crawlspace, Slab, Unfinished Walkout Basement

ORDER ONLINE @ EPLANS.COM

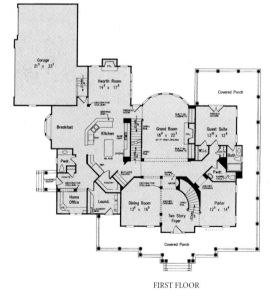

FIRST FLOOR

SECOND FLOOR

FOR MORE DETAILED INFORMATION, PLEASE CHECK THE FLOOR PLANS CAREFULLY.

plan # HPK1900150

First Floor: 2,086 sq. ft.
Second Floor: 1,077 sq. ft.
Total: 3,163 sq. ft.
Bonus Space: 403 sq. ft.
Bedrooms: 4
Bathrooms: 3½
Width: 81' - 10"
Depth: 51' - 8"

ORDER ONLINE @ EPLANS.COM

REAR EXTERIOR

This beautiful farmhouse, with its prominent twin gables and bays, adds just the right amount of country style. The master suite is quietly tucked away downstairs with no rooms directly above. The family cook will love the spacious U-shaped kitchen and adjoining bayed breakfast nook. A bonus room awaits expansion on the second floor, where three large bedrooms share two full baths. Storage space abounds with walk-ins, half-shelves, and linen closets. A curved balcony borders a versatile loft/study, which overlooks the stunning two-story family room.

SECOND FLOOR

FIRST FLOOR

COUNTRY ESTATES

Within the stuccoed walls of this sprawling Southern farmhouse lies the perfect getaway for today's professional family. Whether a weekend refuge or a place to come home to each night, this plan boasts every amenity you could desire. Guests are sure to be impressed by the graceful symmetry of the columned facade and the twin fireplaces in the formal front rooms. A butler's pantry leading from the gourmet kitchen will make service a breeze. A third fireplace in the family room awaits cozier gatherings. A wall of arch-topped windows spans the family room and skylit breakfast room, offering a front row seat to the changing of seasons. When bedtime comes, retreat to the luxurious master suite, secluded in a quiet corner. Three upstairs bedrooms provide plenty of room for kids and guests, and if they're not ready for bed, bonus space for a rec room and a media room occupies the floors above the two garages.

plan# HPK1900151

First Floor: 2,722 sq. ft.
Second Floor: 1,824 sq. ft.
Total: 4,546 sq. ft.
Bonus Space: 802 sq. ft.
Bedrooms: 4
Bathrooms: 3½
Width: 99' - 8"
Depth: 71' - 8"
Foundation: Crawlspace

ORDER ONLINE @ EPLANS.COM

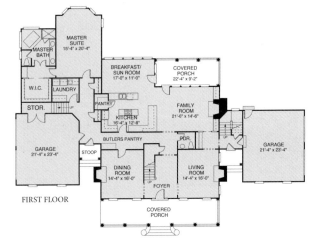

FIRST FLOOR

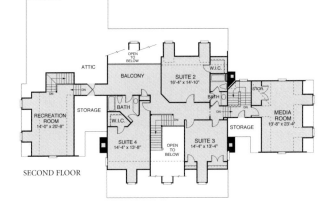

SECOND FLOOR

ORDER BLUEPRINTS 24 HOURS, 7 DAYS A WEEK, AT 1-800-521-6797

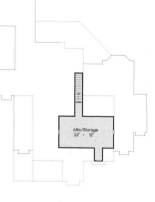

plan # HPK1900152

First Floor: 2,376 sq. ft.

Second Floor: 1,078 sq. ft.

Total: 3,454 sq. ft.

Bonus Space: 549 sq. ft.

Bedrooms: 3

Bathrooms: 2½

Width: 80' - 6"

Depth: 85' - 6"

Foundation: Slab

ORDER ONLINE @ EPLANS.COM

An abundance of muntin windows and a shingle facade are the defining characteristics of this design. Inside, the dining room is graced with French doors to the covered front porch. A home office flanks the foyer on the right. The master bedroom boasts a full bath, His and Hers walk-in closets, and French-door access to the rear covered porch. The grand room flows into the nook and kitchen. The second level holds two family bedrooms that share a lavish walk-through bath. A large future bonus room and a loft complete this level. The third floor houses a spacious attic/storage room.

FIRST FLOOR

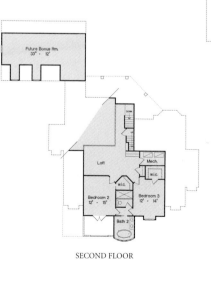

SECOND FLOOR

A wraparound porch makes this unique Victorian farmhouse stand out with style and grace, as does the lovely detailing of this plan. This design is versatile enough to accommodate either a small or large family. The entry is flanked on the left side by a large kitchen/breakfast area with an island, and on the right side by a parlor/music room. The family room is enhanced with a bar ledge, fireplace, and built-in entertainment center. The master suite has access to a covered deck. The upstairs level is shared by three bedrooms, two full baths, and a bonus room. A 448-square-foot apartment is located over the garage.

plan # HPK1900153

First Floor: 2,023 sq. ft.
Second Floor: 749 sq. ft.
Total: 2,772 sq. ft.
Bonus Space: 242 sq. ft.
Bedrooms: 4
Bathrooms: 3½
Width: 77' - 2"
Depth: 57' - 11"
Foundation: Slab, Unfinished Basement

ORDER ONLINE @ EPLANS.COM

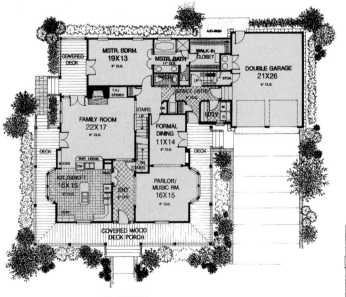

FIRST FLOOR

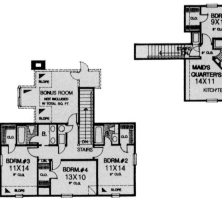

SECOND FLOOR

ORDER BLUEPRINTS 24 HOURS, 7 DAYS A WEEK, AT 1-800-521-6797

plan# HPK1900154

First Floor: 2,027 sq. ft.
Second Floor: 1,430 sq. ft.
Total: 3,457 sq. ft.
Bedrooms: 3
Bathrooms: 3
Width: 98' - 7"
Depth: 72' - 6"
Foundation: Crawlspace

ORDER ONLINE @ EPLANS.COM

A glorious Queen Anne-style exterior hides all the requirements of a modern lifestyle as well as some charming features of earlier times. An octagonal tower is the focal point of the home, housing a unique entry hall. The hall opens to the living room, where a gas fireplace nestles into a corner between banks of windows. A built-in hutch highlights the dining room, and bookshelves slide open to reveal a secret stair leading to the second floor laundry! Other surprises include a discreet four-car garage and a mudroom to collect the clutter of today's busy families. The large kitchen, with a second sink in its central island, easily accommodates multiple cooks. Informal meals can be served on the terrace or in the sunny nook, which opens to the family room. This voluminous space is enhanced by a 14-foot ceiling and walls of windows. Upstairs, the master suite enjoys a corner fireplace, tower sitting room, and private deck.

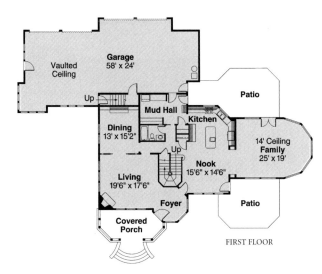

FIRST FLOOR

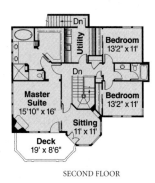

SECOND FLOOR

With both farmhouse flavor and Victorian details, this plan features a wraparound veranda and a bayed area on the first and second floors as well as a turret on the second floor. Inside, the living room's many windows pour light in. The dining area begins with a bay window and is conveniently near the kitchen and breakfast area—also with a bay window. The U-shaped kitchen features an island workstation, ensuring plenty of space for cooking projects. A nearby lavatory is available for guests. The family room has an eye-catching corner-set fireplace. Upstairs, three family bedrooms share a full hall bath, while the master suite has a private bath and balcony, a large walk-in closet, and a sitting alcove, placed within the turret.

plan# HPK1900155

First Floor: 1,155 sq. ft.
Second Floor: 1,209 sq. ft.
Total: 2,364 sq. ft.
Bedrooms: 4
Bathrooms: 2½
Width: 46' - 0"
Depth: 36' - 8"
Foundation: Unfinished Basement

ORDER ONLINE @ EPLANS.COM

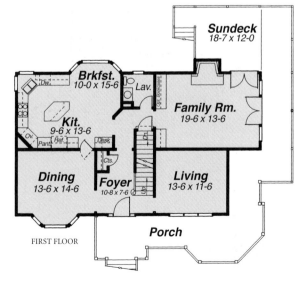

FIRST FLOOR

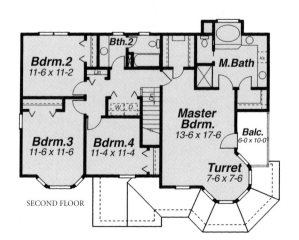

SECOND FLOOR

ORDER BLUEPRINTS 24 HOURS, 7 DAYS A WEEK, AT 1-800-521-6797

plan# HPK1900156

First Floor: 1,362 sq. ft.
Second Floor: 1,270 sq. ft.
Total: 2,632 sq. ft.
Bedrooms: 4
Bathrooms: 2½
Width: 79' - 0"
Depth: 44' - 0"
Foundation: Unfinished Basement,
Crawlspace

ORDER ONLINE @ EPLANS.COM

Rich with Victorian details—scalloped shingles, a wraparound veranda, and turrets—this beautiful facade conceals a modern floor plan. Archways announce a distinctive tray-ceilinged living room and help define the dining room. An octagonal den across from the foyer provides a private spot for reading or studying. The U-shaped island kitchen holds an octagonal breakfast bay and a pass-through breakfast bar to the family room. Upstairs, three family bedrooms share a hall bath—one bedroom is within a turret. The master suite is complete with a bayed sitting room, along with a fancy bath set in another of the turrets.

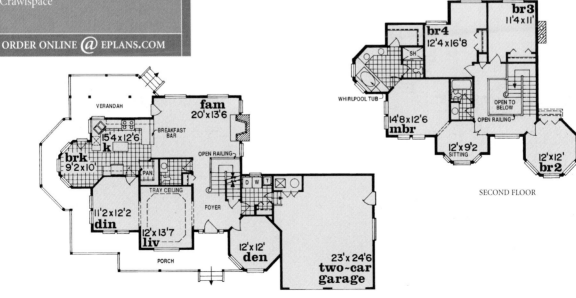

SECOND FLOOR

FIRST FLOOR

With details reminiscent of Victorian design, this home is graced by a covered veranda wrapping on three sides and an elegant bay window. The vaulted foyer introduces an octagonal staircase and an archway to the living room. Details in the living room include a tray ceiling and adjoining dining room with beam ceiling. French doors in the dining room open to the porch. A country kitchen offers a spacious walk-in pantry, a center prep island, and a breakfast bay with porch access. The nearby family room has its own fireplace. The upstairs master bedroom is graced by a bayed sitting area and bath with private deck. Bedrooms 2, 3, and 4 share the use of a full hall bath. A railed gallery on the second floor overlooks the foyer below and is brightened by the bay windows.

plan# HPK1900157

First Floor: 1,205 sq. ft.
Second Floor: 1,254 sq. ft.
Total: 2,459 sq. ft.
Bedrooms: 4
Bathrooms: 2½
Width: 71' - 6"
Depth: 56' - 6"
Foundation: Crawlspace, Unfinished Basement

ORDER ONLINE @ EPLANS.COM

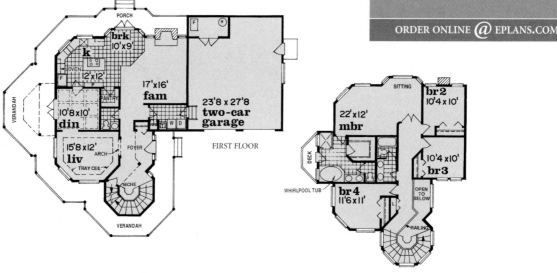

FIRST FLOOR

SECOND FLOOR

plan# HPK1900158

First Floor: 2,347 sq. ft.
Second Floor: 1,087 sq. ft.
Total: 3,434 sq. ft.
Bedrooms: 4
Bathrooms: 2½
Width: 93' - 6"
Depth: 61' - 0"
Foundation: Unfinished Basement

ORDER ONLINE @ EPLANS.COM

Dutch-gable rooflines and a gabled wraparound porch provide an extra measure of farmhouse style. The foyer opens on the left to the study or guest bedroom that leads to the master suite. To the right is the formal dining room; the massive great room is in the center. The kitchen combines with the great room, the breakfast nook, and the dining room for entertaining options. The master suite includes access to the covered patio, a spacious walk-in closet, and a full bath with a whirlpool tub.

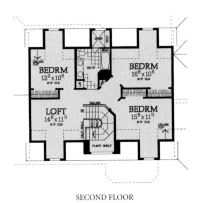

SECOND FLOOR

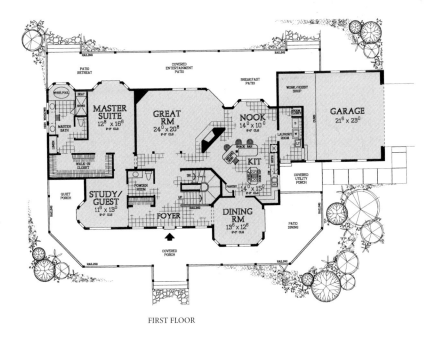

FIRST FLOOR

© William E. Poole Designs, Inc.

This Colonial farmhouse will be the showpiece of your neighborhood. Come in from the wide front porch through French doors topped by a sunburst window. Continue past the formal dining and living rooms to a columned gallery and a large family room with a focal fireplace. The kitchen astounds with a unique layout, an island, and abundant counter and cabinet space. The master bath balances luxury with efficiency. Three upstairs bedrooms enjoy amenities such as dormer windows or walk-in closets. Bonus space is ready for expansion as your needs change.

plan# HPK1900159

First Floor: 2,191 sq. ft.
Second Floor: 1,220 sq. ft.
Total: 3,411 sq. ft.
Bonus Space: 280 sq. ft.
Bedrooms: 4
Bathrooms: 3½
Width: 75' - 8"
Depth: 54' - 4"
Foundation: Crawlspace, Unfinished Basement

ORDER ONLINE @ EPLANS.COM

FIRST FLOOR

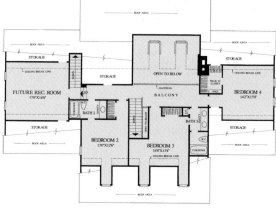

SECOND FLOOR

plan # HPK1900160

First Floor: 3,170 sq. ft.
Second Floor: 1,914 sq. ft.
Total: 5,084 sq. ft.
Bonus Space: 445 sq. ft.
Bedrooms: 4
Bathrooms: 3½
Width: 100' - 10"
Depth: 65' - 5"
Foundation: Crawlspace

ORDER ONLINE @ EPLANS.COM

This elegantly appointed home is a beauty inside and out. A centerpiece stair rises gracefully from the two-story grand foyer. The kitchen, breakfast room, and family room provide open space for the gathering of family and friends. The beam-ceilinged study and the dining room flank the grand foyer, and each includes a fireplace. The master bedroom features a cozy sitting area and a luxury master bath with His and Hers vanities and walk-in closets. Three large bedrooms and a game room complete the second floor. A large expandable area is available at the top of the rear stair.

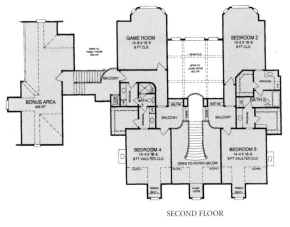

SECOND FLOOR

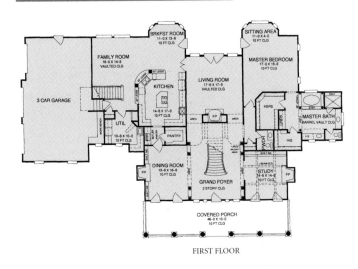

FIRST FLOOR

Subtle Victorian details add charm to this spacious cottage home. A full-length covered porch is topped by twin dormers and an open-face gable. The entry opens to the dining room on the right and a vaulted family room to the back. A fireplace is the focal point of the family room. The breakfast nook adjoins the hardworking island kitchen and vaulted keeping room. The master suite enjoys privacy and all the amenities such as His and Hers walk-in closets and a tray ceiling. The second floor provides three family bedrooms, two full baths, and a computer alcove.

plan# HPK1900161

First Floor: 2,182 sq. ft.
Second Floor: 980 sq. ft.
Total: 3,162 sq. ft.
Bedrooms: 4
Bathrooms: 3½
Width: 70' - 4"
Depth: 65' - 0"
Foundation: Crawlspace, Unfinished Walkout Basement, Slab

ORDER ONLINE @ EPLANS.COM

FIRST FLOOR

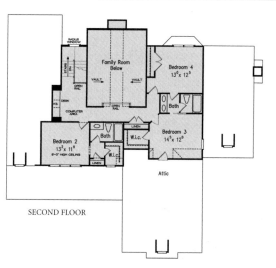

SECOND FLOOR

ORDER BLUEPRINTS 24 HOURS, 7 DAYS A WEEK, AT 1-800-521-6797

plan# HPK1900162

First Floor: 2,113 sq. ft.
Second Floor: 2,098 sq. ft.
Total: 4,211 sq. ft.
Bedrooms: 5
Bathrooms: 4½
Width: 68' - 6"
Depth: 53' - 0"
Foundation: Slab, Unfinished Walkout
Basement, Crawlspace

ORDER ONLINE @ EPLANS.COM

This two-story farmhouse has much to offer, with the most exciting feature being the opulent master suite, which takes up almost the entire width of the upper level. French doors access the large master bedroom, featuring a coffered ceiling. Steps lead to a separate sitting room with a fireplace and sun-filled bay window. His and Hers walk-in closets lead the way to a vaulted private bath with separate vanities and a lavish whirlpool tub. On the first floor, an island kitchen and a bayed breakfast room flow into a two-story family room with a raised-hearth fireplace, built-in shelves, and French-door access to the rear yard.

SECOND FLOOR

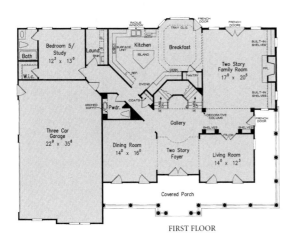

FIRST FLOOR

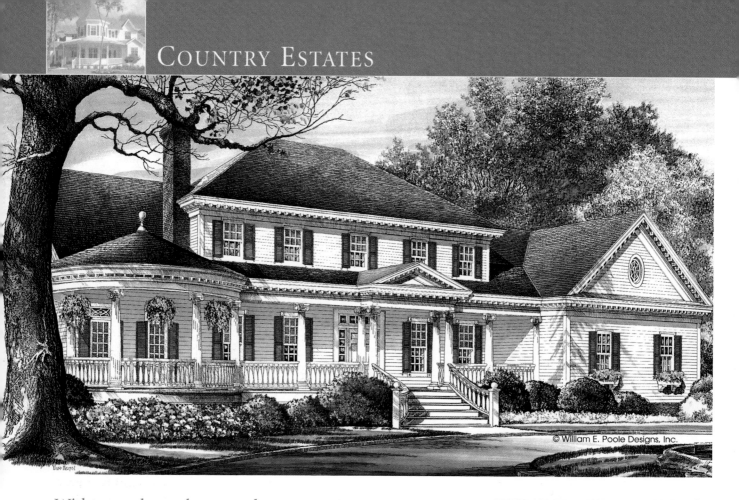

© William E. Poole Designs, Inc.

With a gazebo-style covered porch and careful exterior details, you can't help but imagine tea parties, porch swings, and lazy summer evenings. Inside, a living room/library will comfort with its fireplace and built-ins. The family room is graced with a fireplace and a curved, two-story ceiling with an overlook above. The master bedroom is a private retreat with a lovely bath, twin walk-in closets, and rear-porch access. Upstairs, three bedrooms with sizable closets—one bedroom would make an excellent guest suite or alternate master suite—share access to expandable space.

plan# HPK1900163

First Floor: 2,442 sq. ft.
Second Floor: 1,286 sq. ft.
Total: 3,728 sq. ft.
Bonus Space: 681 sq. ft.
Bedrooms: 4
Bathrooms: 3½ + ½
Width: 84' - 8"
Depth: 60' - 0"
Foundation: Crawlspace

ORDER ONLINE @ EPLANS.COM

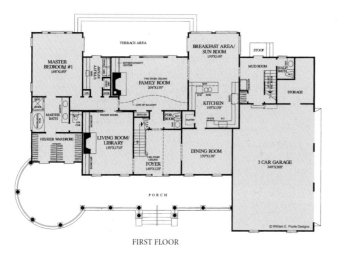

FIRST FLOOR

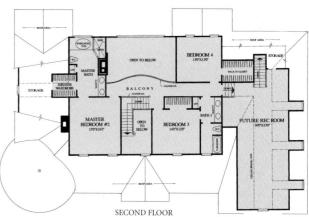

SECOND FLOOR

plan# HPK1900164

First Floor: 1,992 sq. ft.
Second Floor: 1,458 sq. ft.
Total: 3,450 sq. ft.
Bonus Space: 380 sq. ft.
Bedrooms: 5
Bathrooms: 3½
Width: 108' - 0"
Depth: 64' - 0"
Foundation: Unfinished Basement

ORDER ONLINE @ EPLANS.COM

The origin of this house dates back to 1787 and George Washington's stately Mount Vernon. The unusual design features curved galleries leading to matching wings. In the main house, the living and dining rooms provide a large open area, with access to the rear porch for additional entertaining possibilities. A keeping room features a pass-through to the kitchen and a fireplace with a built-in wood box. Four bedrooms, including a master suite with a fireplace, are found upstairs. One wing contains separate guest quarters with a full bath, a lounge area, and an upstairs studio, which features a spiral staircase and a loft area. On the other side of the house, the second floor over the garage can be used for storage or as a hobby room.

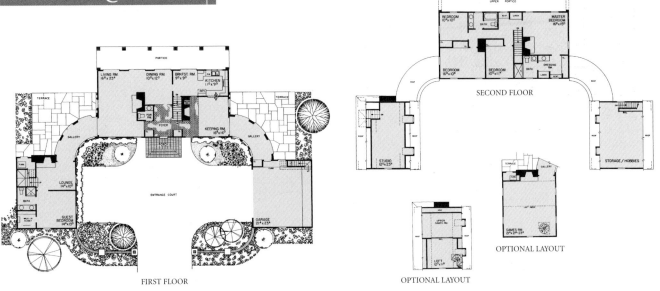

FIRST FLOOR

SECOND FLOOR

OPTIONAL LAYOUT

OPTIONAL LAYOUT

At nearly 5,200 square feet, this French Country beauty is replete with luxurious amenities inside that match the elegance outside. Formal living spaces are made contemporary with upgraded ceiling treatments and abundant space. The expansive great room is ideal for social gatherings with convenient access to the rear porch. To the left, the first-floor master bedroom enjoys privacy and seclusion. Upstairs, the three family bedrooms each boast a full bath. Friends and family alike will indulge in the ever popular media room. The half-bath adjacent to the media room is a thoughtful accomodation for guests. A discreet, side-loading three-car garage adds curb appeal.

plan# HPK1900165

First Floor: 2,864 sq. ft.
Second Floor: 2,329 sq. ft.
Total: 5,193 sq. ft.
Bedrooms: 4
Bathrooms: 4½ + ½
Width: 64' - 6"
Depth: 87' - 6"
Foundation: Unfinished Walkout Basement

ORDER ONLINE @ EPLANS.COM

FIRST FLOOR

SECOND FLOOR

plan# HPK1900166

First Floor: 2,729 sq. ft.
Second Floor: 1,157 sq. ft.
Total: 3,886 sq. ft.
Bedrooms: 4
Bathrooms: 3½
Width: 73' - 11"
Depth: 70' - 11"
Foundation: Unfinished Basement

ORDER ONLINE @ EPLANS.COM

Fieldstone, cedar shakes, and gentle curves reflect this country home's pastoral nature. Situated at the top of a valley, it will reward you with views from nearly every room. The two-story grand room features a curved wall of floor-to-ceiling windows; when night obscures the view, turn your attention to the magnificent fireplace flanked by built-in media cabinets. The panorama continues in the breakfast room and on into the hearth-warmed family room. An open floor plan ensures that the light and the views can be experienced from the spectacular gourmet kitchen as well. Enjoy the ambiance in a more intimate setting by retreating to the master suite, where a third fireplace is centered in a windowed bay. One more fireplace can be found in the study, which also features a curved window wall and built-in cabinetry. An upstairs loft offers another perspective of the grand room's light and views.

FIRST FLOOR

SECOND FLOOR

Open gables with light-catching windows, shed dormers, and stone detailing combine to create an unbeatable Craftsman-influenced facade. The foyer is surrounded by the dining room, study, and living room—find the first of two fireplaces here. The spacious and inviting kitchen is a dream come true—and notice the door leading outside for easy grocery unloading. An office is tucked away near the utility room. The master suite is conveniently located on the first floor, occupying the left side of the home and enjoying dual walk-in closets and a fantastic bath. Three more bedrooms—each with a walk-in closet—reside upstairs.

plan # HPK1900167

First Floor: 2,589 sq. ft.
Second Floor: 981 sq. ft.
Total: 3,570 sq. ft.
Bedrooms: 4
Bathrooms: 3½
Width: 70' - 8"
Depth: 61' - 10"
Foundation: Crawlspace

ORDER ONLINE @ EPLANS.COM

FIRST FLOOR

SECOND FLOOR

ORDER BLUEPRINTS 24 HOURS, 7 DAYS A WEEK, AT 1-800-521-6797

plan # HPK1900168

Main Level: 2,932 sq. ft.
Lower Level: 1,556 sq. ft.
Total: 4,488 sq. ft.
Bedrooms: 3
Bathrooms: 3½ + ½
Width: 114' - 0"
Depth: 82' - 11"
Foundation: Finished Walkout
Basement

ORDER ONLINE @ EPLANS.COM

The interior of this home boasts high ceilings, a wealth of windows, and interestingly shaped rooms. A covered portico leads into a roomy foyer, which is flanked by an office/study, accessible through French doors. Just beyond the foyer, a huge, vaulted family room highlights columns decorating the entrance and positioned throughout the room. The island kitchen nestles close to the beautiful dining room, which features rear property views through the bay window and a nearby door to the terrace. The main-level master suite enjoys two walk-in closets and a lavish bath, as well as access to a covered terrace. The lower level is home to the remaining bedrooms, including suites 2 and 3, an abundance of storage, a recreation room, and a large mechanical/storage room.

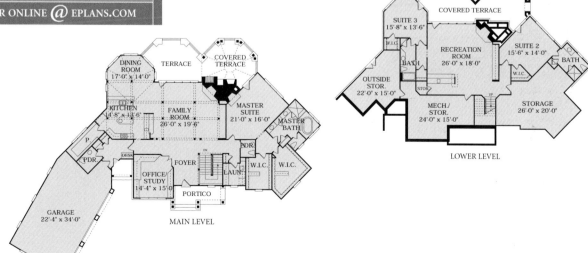

MAIN LEVEL

LOWER LEVEL

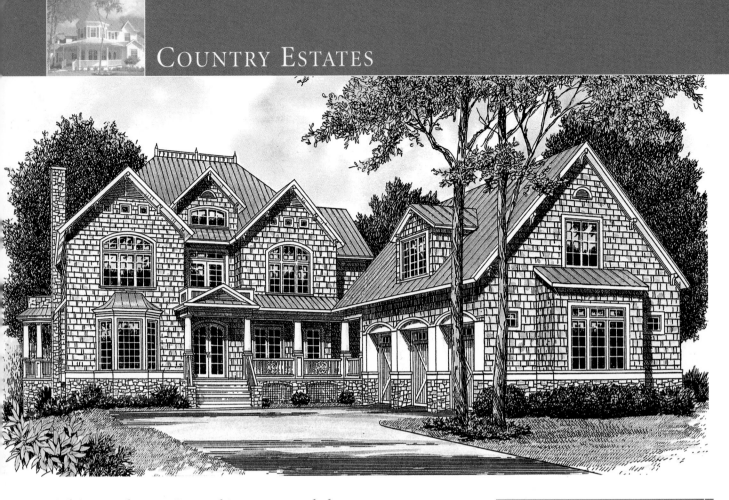

This Northwest Coastal/country-style home extends livability outside with its front and back porches and elevated deck. The first floor flows from the open family room and breakfast nook to the kitchen with U-shaped counters. The dining room opens to the kitchen and the foyer. In the front, a guest suite contains a private bath. Upstairs, the spacious master bedroom has a walk-in closet and access to the deck. The family bedrooms share a bath with the study. Attached to the main house by a breezeway, the garage includes an unfinished area above that can be converted to an apartment.

plan# HPK1900169

First Floor: 2,030 sq. ft.
Second Floor: 1,967 sq. ft.
Third Floor: 642 sq. ft.
Total: 4,685 sq. ft.
Bedrooms: 4
Bathrooms: 5
Width: 80' - 8"
Depth: 111' - 8"
Foundation: Crawlspace

ORDER ONLINE @ EPLANS.COM

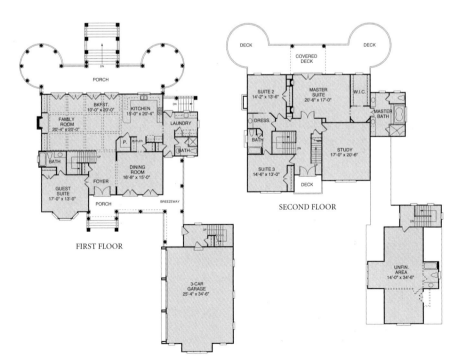

FIRST FLOOR

SECOND FLOOR

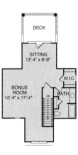

plan # HPK1900170

First Floor: 2,215 sq. ft.

Second Floor: 708 sq. ft.

Total: 2,923 sq. ft.

Bonus Space: 420 sq. ft.

Bedrooms: 3

Bathrooms: 3

Width: 76' - 4"

Depth: 69' - 10"

Foundation: Crawlspace

ORDER ONLINE @ EPLANS.COM

Clean, simple lines define this Victorian-style home, which opens through double doors to a spacious grand room. Adornments here include a coffered ceiling and triple French doors to the covered porch at the back. Both the dining room and the master bedroom feature stepped ceilings. Two walk-in closets and a fine bath with a separate tub and shower further enhance the master suite. Both family bedrooms upstairs have walk-in closets and built-ins. A bonus room can become an additional bedroom later, with space for a full bath.

FIRST FLOOR

SECOND FLOOR

© THE SATER DESIGN COLLECTION, INC.

Turn Your
Dream Home
Into A *Reality*

Finding the right
new home to fit

▶ Your style
▶ Your budget
▶ Your life

...has never
been easier.

Our house plan collections offers
distinctive design coupled with
plans to match every wallet. If
you are looking to build your new
home, look to Hanley Wood first.

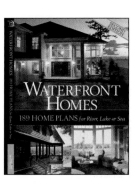

WATERFRONT HOMES
1-931131-28-7

$10.95 (208 PAGES)

A collection of gorgeous homes
for those who dream of life
on the water's edge—this title
features open floor plans with
expansive views.

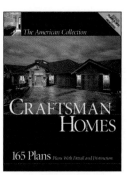

AMERICAN COLLECTION:
CRAFTSMAN
978-1-931131-54-4

$10.95 (192 PAGES)

Celebrate the fine details and modest proportions of the Craftsman
style with this beautiful collection of
165 homes.

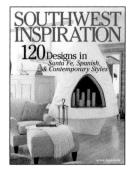

SOUTHWEST INSPIRATION
1-931131-19-8

$14.95 (192 PAGES)

This title features 120 designs
in Santa Fe, Spanish and
Contemporary styles.

MEDITERRANEAN
INSPIRATION
1-931131-09-0

$14.95 (192 PAGES)

Bring home the timeless beauty
of the Mediterranean with the
gorgeous plans featured in this popular title.

One Thomas Circle, N.W, Suite 600, Washington, DC 20005

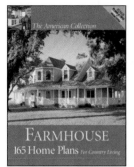

AMERICAN COLLECTION: FARMHOUSE
978-1-931131-55-1

$10.95 (192 PAGES)

Homes with gabled roofs, wood, stone or glass themes, wrap-around porches and open floorplans make up this wonderful assortment of farmhouse plans.

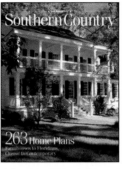

SOUTHERN COUNTRY, 2ND ED.
1-881955-89-3

$13.95 (263 PAGES)

Southern Country Home Plans showcases 300 plans from Historic Colonials to Contemporary Coastals.

PROVENCAL INSPIRATION
1-881955-89-3

$14.95 (192 PAGES)

This title features home plans, landscapes and interior plans that evoke the French Country spirit.

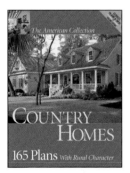

THE AMERICAN COLLECTION: COUNTRY HOMES
1-931131-35-X

$10.95 (192 PAGES)

The American Collection: Country is a must-have if you're looking to build a country home or if you want to bring the relaxed country spirit into your current home.

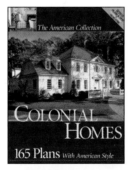

THE AMERICAN COLLECTION: COLONIAL HOMES
1-931131-40-6

$10.95 (192 PAGES)

This beautiful collection features distinctly American home styles— find everything from Colonials, Cape Cod, Georgian, Farmhouse to Saltbox.

PICK UP A COPY TODAY!

Toll-Free:
877.447.5450

Online:
www.hanleywoodbooks.com

Hanley Wood provides the largest selection of plans from the nation's top designers and architects. Our special home styles collection offers designs to suit any style.

HANLEY WOOD

One Thomas Circle, NW, Suite 600, Washington, DC 20005

ACF1

With more than 50 years of experience in the industry and millions of blueprints sold, Hanley Wood is a trusted source of high-quality, high-value pre-drawn home plans.

Using pre-drawn home plans is a **reliable, cost-effective way** to build your dream home, and our vast selection of plans is second-to-none. The nation's finest designers craft these plans that builders know they can trust. Meanwhile, our friendly, knowledgeable customer service representatives can help you every step of the way.

WHAT YOU'LL GET WITH YOUR ORDER

The contents of each designer's blueprint package is unique, but all contain detailed, high-quality working drawings. You can expect to find the following standard elements in most sets of plans:

1. FRONT PERSPECTIVE

This artist's sketch of the exterior of the house gives you an idea of how the house will look when built and landscaped.

4. HOUSE AND DETAIL CROSS-SECTIONS

Large-scale views show sections or cutaways of the foundation, interior walls, exterior walls, floors, stairways, and roof details. Additional cross-sections may show important changes in floor, ceiling, or roof heights, or the relationship of one level to another. These sections show exactly how the various parts of the house fit together and are extremely valuable during construction. Additional sheets may include enlarged wall, floor, and roof construction details.

2. FOUNDATION AND BASEMENT PLANS

This sheet shows the foundation layout including concrete walls, footings, pads, posts, beams, bearing walls, and foundation notes. If the home features a basement, the first-floor framing details may also be included on this plan. If your plan features slab construction rather than a basement, the plan shows footings and details for a monolithic slab. This page, or another in the set, may include a sample plot plan for locating your house on a building site. Additional sheets focus on foundation cross-sections and other details.

3. DETAILED FLOOR PLANS

These plans show the layout of each floor of the house. Rooms and interior spaces are carefully dimensioned, doors and windows located, and keys are given for cross-section details provided elsewhere in the plans.

5. FLOOR STRUCTURAL SUPPORTS

The floor framing plans provide detail for these crucial elements of your home. Each includes floor joist, ceiling joist, spacing, direction, span, and specifications. Beam and window headers, along with necessary details for framing connections, stairways, or dormers are also included.

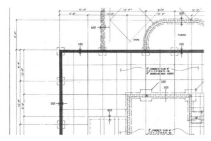

6. ELECTRICAL PLAN
The electrical plan offers suggested locations with notes for all lighting, outlets, switches, and circuits. A layout is provided for each level, as well as basements, garages, or other structures. This plan does not contain diagrams detailing how all wiring should be run, or how circuits should be engineered. These details should be designed by your electrician.

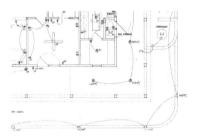

7. EXTERIOR ELEVATIONS
In addition to the front exterior, your blueprint set will include drawings of the rear and sides of your house as well. These drawings give notes on exterior materials and finishes. Particular attention is given to cornice detail, brick and stone accents, or other finish items that make your home unique.

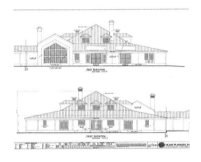

ROOF FRAMING PLANS — PLEASE READ
Some plans contain roof framing plans; however because of the wide variation in local requirements, many plans do not. If you buy a plan without a roof framing plan, you will need an engineer familiar with local building codes to create a plan to build your roof. Even if your plan does contain a roof framing plan, we recommend that a local engineer review the plan to verify that it will meet local codes.

BEFORE YOU CALL

You are making a terrific decision to use a pre-drawn house plan—it is one you can make with confidence, knowing that your blueprints are crafted by national-award-winning certified residential designers and architects, and trusted by builders.

Once you've selected the plan you want—or even if you have questions along the way—our experienced customer service representatives are available 24 hours a day, seven days a week to help you navigate the home-building process. To help them provide you with even better service, please consider the following questions before you call:

■ Have you chosen or purchased your lot?
If so, please review the building setback requirements of your local building authority before you call. You don't need to have a lot before ordering plans, but if you own land already, please have the width and depth dimensions handy when you call.

■ Have you chosen a builder?
Involving your builder in the plan selection and evaluation process may be beneficial. Luckily, builders know they can have confidence with pre-drawn plans because they've been designed for livability, functionality, and typically are builder-proven at successful home sites across the country.

■ Do you need a construction loan?
Construction loans are unique because they involve determining the value of something that is not yet constructed. Several lenders offer convenient contstruction-to-permanent loans. It is important to choose a good lending partner—one who will help guide you through the application and appraisal process. Most will even help you evaluate your contractor to ensure reliability and credit worthiness. Our partnership with IndyMac Bank, a nationwide leader in construction loans, can help you save on your loan, if needed (see the next page for details).

■ How many sets of plans do you need?
Building a home can typically require a number of sets of blueprints—one for yourself, two or three for the builder and subcontractors, two for the local building department, and one or more for your lender. For this reason, we offer 5- and 8-set plan packages, but your best value is the Reproducible Plan Package. Reproducible plans are accompanied by a license to make modifications and typically up to 12 duplicates of the plan so you have enough copies of the plan for everyone involved in the financing and construction of your home.

■ Do you want to make any changes to the plan?
We understand that it is difficult to find blueprints for a home that will meet all of your needs. That is why Hanley Wood is glad to offer plan Customization Services. We will work with you to design the modifications you'd like to see and to adjust your blueprint plans accordingly—anything from changing the foundation; adding square footage, redesigning baths, kitchens, or bedrooms; or most other modifications. This simple, cost-effective service saves you from hiring an outside architect to make alterations. Modifications may only be made to Reproducible Plan Packages that include the license to modify.

■ Do you have to make any changes to meet local building codes?
While all of our plans are drawn to meet national building codes at the time they were created, many areas required that plans be stamped by a local engineer to certify that they meet local building codes. Building codes are updated frequently and can vary by state, county, city, or municipality. Contact your local building inspection department, office of planning and zoning, or department of permits to determine how your local codes will affect your construction project. The best way to assure that you can make changes to your plan, if necessary, is to purchase a Reproducible Plan Package.

■ Has everyone—from family members to contractors—been involved in selecting the plan?
Building a new home is an exciting process, and using pre-drawn plans is a great way to realize your dreams. Make sure that everyone involved has had an opportunity to review the plan you've selected. While Hanley Wood is the only plans provider with an exchange policy, it's best to be sure all parties agree on your selection before you buy.

CALL TOLL-FREE 1-800-521-6797
Source Key HPK19

CUSTOMIZE YOUR PLAN – HANLEY WOOD CUSTOMIZATION SERVICES

Creating custom home plans has never been easier and more directly accessible. Using state-of-the-art technology and top-performing architectural expertise, Hanley Wood delivers on a long-standing customer commitment to provide world-class home-plans and customization services. Our valued customers—professional home builders and individual home owners—appreciate the convenience and accessibility of this interactive, consultative service.

With the Hanley Wood Customization Service you can:

■ Save valuable time by avoiding drawn-out and frequently repetitive face-to-face design meetings

■ Communicate design and home-plan changes faster and more efficiently
■ Speed-up project turn-around time
■ Build on a budget without sacrificing quality
■ Transform master home plans to suit your design needs and unique personal style

All of our design options and prices are impressively affordable. A detailed quote is available for a $50 consultation fee. Plan modification is an interactive service. Our skilled team of designers will guide you through the customization process from start to finish making recommendations, offering ideas, and determining the feasibility of your changes. This level of service is offered to ensure the final modified plan meets your expectations. If you use our service the $50 fee will be applied to the cost of the modifications.

You may purchase the customization consultation before or after purchasing a plan. In either case, it is necessary to purchase the Reproducible Plan Package and complete the accompanying license to modify the plan before we can begin customization.

Customization Consultation $50

TOOLS TO WORK WITH YOUR BUILDER

Two Reverse Options For Your Convenience – Mirror and Right-Reading Reverse (as available)

Mirror reverse plans simply flip the design 180 degrees—keep in mind, the text will also be flipped. For a minimal fee you can have one or all of your plans shipped mirror reverse, although we recommend having at least one regular set handy. Right-reading reverse plans show the design flipped 180 degrees but the text reads normally. When you choose this option, we ship each set of purchased blueprints in this format.

Mirror Reverse Fee (indicate the number of sets when ordering) $55
Right Reading Reverse Fee (all sets are reversed) $175

A Shopping List Exclusively for Your Home – Materials List

A customized Materials List helps you plan and estimate the cost of your new home, outlining the quantity, type, and size of materials needed to build your house (with the exception of mechanical system items). Included are framing lumber, windows and doors, kitchen and bath cabinetry, rough and finished hardware, and much more.

Materials List . . . .$75 each
Additional Materials Lists (at original time of purchase only)$20 each

Plan Your Home-Building Process – Specification Outline

Work with your builder on this step-by-step chronicle of 166 stages or items crucial to the building process. It provides a comprehensive review of the construction process and helps you choose materials.
Specification Outline . . . .$10 each

Get Accurate Cost Estimates for Your Home – Quote One® Cost Reports

The Summary Cost Report, the first element in the Quote One® package, breaks down the cost of your home into various categories based on building materials, labor, and installation, and includes three grades of construction: Budget, Standard, and Custom. Make even more informed decisions about your project with the second element of our package, the Material Cost Report. The material and installation cost is shown for each of more than 1,000 line items provided in the standard-grade Materials List, which is included with this tool. Additional space is included for estimates from contractors and subcontractors, such as for mechanical materials, which are not included in our packages.

Quote One® Summary Cost Report $35
Quote One® Detailed Material Cost Report $140*
***Detailed material cost report includes the Materials List**

Learn the Basics of Building – Electrical, Pluming, Mechanical, Construction Detail Sheets

If you want to know more about building techniques—and deal more confidently with your subcontractors—we offer four useful detail sheets. These sheets provide non-plan-specific general information, but are excellent tools that will add to your understanding of Plumbing Details, Electrical Details, Construction Details, and Mechanical Details.

Electrical Detail Sheet $14.95
Plumbing Detail Sheet $14.95
Mechanical Detail Sheet $14.95
Construction Detail Sheet $14.95
SUPER VALUE SETS:
Buy any 2: $26.95; Buy any 3: $34.95; Buy All 4 $39.95

Best Value

GETTY IMAGES (2)

MAKE YOUR HOME TECH-READY – HOME AUTOMATION UPGRADE

Building a new home provides a unique opportunity to wire it with a plan for future needs. A Home Automation-Ready (HA-Ready) home contains the wiring substructure of tomorrow's connected home. It means that every room—from the front porch to the backyard, and from the attic to the basement—is wired for security, lighting, telecommunications, climate control, home computer networking, whole-house audio, home theater, shade control, video surveillance, entry access control, and yes, video gaming electronic solutions.

Along with the conveniences HA-Ready homes provide, they also have a higher resale value. The Consumer Electronics Association (CEA), in conjunction with the Custom Electronic Design and Installation Association (CEDIA), have developed a TechHome™ Rating system that quantifies the value of HA-Ready homes. The rating system is gaining widespread recognition in the real estate industry.

Developed by CEDIA-certified installers, our Home Automation Upgrade package includes everything you need to work with an installer during the construction of your home. It provides a short explanation of the various subsystems, a wiring floor plan for each level of your home, a detailed materials list with estimated costs, and a list of CEDIA-certified installers in your local area.
Home Automation Upgrade $250

GET YOUR HOME PLANS PAID FOR!

IndyMac Bank, in partnership with Hanley Wood, will reimburse you up to $600 toward the cost of your home plans simply by financing the construction of your new home with IndyMac Bank Home Construction Lending.

IndyMac's construction and permanent loan is a one-time close loan, meaning that one application—and one set of closing fees—provides all the financing you need.

Apply today at www.indymacbank.com, call toll free at 1-866-237-3478, or ask a Hanley Wood customer service representative for details.

DESIGN YOUR HOME – INTERIOR AND EXTERIOR FINISHING TOUCHES

Be Your Own Interior Designer! – Home Furniture Planner

Effectively plan the space in your home using our Hands-On Home Furniture Planner. It's fun and easy—no more moving heavy pieces of furniture to see how the room will go together. The kit includes reusable peel-and-stick furniture templates that fit on a 12"x18" laminated layout board—enough space to lay out every room in your house.
Home Furniture Planning Kit $15.95

Enjoy the Outdoors! – Deck Plans

Many of our homes have a corresponding deck plan, sold separately, which includes a Deck Plan Frontal Sheet, Deck Framing and Floor Plans, Deck Elevations, and a Deck Materials List. A Standard Deck Details Package, also available, provides all the how-to information necessary for building any deck. Get both the Deck Plan and the Standard Deck Details Package for one low price in our Complete Deck Building Package. See the price tier chart below and call for deck plan availability.
Deck Details (only) $14.95
Deck Building Package . . . . Plan price + $14.95

Create a Professionally Designed Landscape – Landscape Plans

Many of our homes have a front-yard Landscape Plan that is complementary in design to the house plan. These comprehensive Landscape Blueprint Packages include a Frontal Sheet, Plan View, Regionalized Plant & Materials List, a sheet on Planting and Maintaining Your Landscape, Zone Maps,  and a Plant Size and Description Guide. Each set of blueprints is a full 18" x 24" with clear, complete instructions in easy-to-read type. Our Landscape Plans are available with a Plant & Materials List adapted by horticultural experts to eight regions of the country. Please specify your region when ordering your plan—see region map below. Call for more information about landscape plan availability and applicable regions.

LANDSCAPE & DECK PRICE SCHEDULE

PRICE TIERS	1-SET STUDY PACKAGE	5-SET BUILDING PACKAGE	8-SET BUILDING PACKAGE	1-SET REPRODUCIBLE*
P1	$25	$55	$95	$145
P2	$45	$75	$115	$165
P3	$75	$105	$145	$195
P4	$105	$135	$175	$225
P5	$145	$175	$215	$275
P6	$185	$215	$255	$315

PRICES SUBJECT TO CHANGE   * REQUIRES A FAX NUMBER

TERMS & CONDITIONS

OUR 90-DAY EXCHANGE POLICY

BUY WITH CONFIDENCE!

Hanley Wood is committed to ensuring your satisfaction with your blueprint order, which is why we offer a 90-day exchange policy. With the exception of Reproducible Plan Package orders, we will exchange your entire first order for an equal or greater number of blueprints from our plan collection within 90 days of the original order. The entire content of your original order must be returned before an exchange will be processed. Please call our customer service department at 1-888-690-1116 for your return authorization number and shipping instructions. If the returned blueprints look used, redlined, or copied, we will not honor your exchange. Fees for exchanging your blueprints are as follows: 20% of the amount of the original order, plus the difference in cost if exchanging for a design in a higher price bracket or less the difference in cost if exchanging for a design in a lower price bracket. (Because they can be copied, Reproducible blueprints are not exchangeable or refundable.) Please call for current postage and handling prices. Shipping and handling charges are not refundable.

ARCHITECTURAL AND ENGINEERING SEALS

Some cities and states now require that a licensed architect or engineer review and "seal" a blueprint, or officially approve it, prior to construction. Prior to application for a building permit or the start of actual construction, we strongly advise that you consult your local building official who can tell you if such a review is required.

LOCAL BUILDING CODES AND ZONING REQUIREMENTS

Each plan was designed to meet or exceed the requirements of a nationally recognized model building code in effect at the time and place the plan was drawn. Typically plans designed after the year 2000 conform to the International Residential Building Code (IRC 2000 or 2003). The IRC is comprised of portions of the three major codes below. Plans drawn before 2000 conform to one of the three recognized building codes in effect at the time: Building Officials and Code Administrators (BOCA) International, Inc.;

the Southern Building Code Congress International, (SBCCI) Inc.; the International Conference of Building Officials (ICBO); or the Council of American Building Officials (CABO).

Because of the great differences in geography and climate throughout the United States and Canada, each state, county, and municipality has its own building codes, zone requirements, ordinances, and building regulations. Your plan may need to be modified to comply with local requirements. In addition, you may need to obtain permits or inspections from local governments before and in the course of construction. We authorize the use of the blueprints on the express condition that you consult a local licensed architect or engineer of your choice prior to beginning construction and strictly comply with all local building codes, zoning requirements, and other applicable laws, regulations, ordinances, and requirements. Notice: Plans for homes to be built in Nevada must be redrawn by a Nevada-registered professional. Consult your local building official for more information on this subject.

TERMS AND CONDITIONS

These designs are protected under the terms of United States Copyright Law and may not be copied or reproduced in any way, by

any means, unless you have purchased a Reproducible Plan Package and signed the accompanying license to modify and copy the plan, which clearly indicates your right to modify, copy, or reproduce. We authorize the use of your chosen design as an aid in the construction of ONE (1) single- or multifamily home only. You may not use this design to build a second dwelling or multiple dwellings without purchasing another blueprint or blueprints or paying additional design fees. Multi-use fees vary by designer—please call one of experienced sales representatives for a quote.

DISCLAIMER

The designers we work with have put substantial care and effort into the creation of their blueprints. However, because we cannot provide on-site consultation, supervision, and control over actual construction, and because of the great variance in local building requirements, building practices, and soil, seismic, weather, and other conditions, WE MAKE NO WARRANTY OF ANY KIND, EXPRESS OR IMPLIED, WITH RESPECT TO THE CONTENT OR USE OF THE BLUEPRINTS, INCLUDING BUT NOT LIMITED TO ANY WARRANTY OF MERCHANTABILITY OR OF FITNESS FOR A PARTICULAR PURPOSE. ITEMS, PRICES, TERMS, AND CONDITIONS ARE SUBJECT TO CHANGE WITHOUT NOTICE.

CALL TOLL-FREE 1-866-473-4052 OR VISIT EPLANS.COM

IMPORTANT COPYRIGHT NOTICE

From the Council of Publishing Home Designers

Blueprints for residential construction (or working drawings, as they are often called in the industry) are copyrighted intellectual property, protected under the terms of the United States Copyright Law and, therefore, cannot be copied legally for use in building. The following are some guidelines to help you get what you need to build your home, without violating copyright law:

1. HOME PLANS ARE COPYRIGHTED

Just like books, movies, and songs, home plans receive protection under the federal copyright laws. The copyright laws prevent anyone, other than the copyright owner, from reproducing, modifying, or reusing the plans or design without permission of the copyright owner.

2. DO NOT COPY DESIGNS OR FLOOR PLANS FROM ANY PUBLICATION, ELECTRONIC MEDIA, OR EXISTING HOME

It is illegal to copy, change, or redraw home designs found in a plan book, CDROM or on the Internet. The right to modify plans is one of the exclusive rights of copyright. It is also illegal to copy or redraw a constructed home that is protected by copyright, even if you have never seen the plans for the home. If you find a plan or home that you like, you must purchase a set of plans from an authorized source. The plans may not be lent, given away, or sold by the purchaser.

3. DO NOT USE PLANS TO BUILD MORE THAN ONE HOUSE

The original purchaser of house plans is typically licensed to build a single home from the plans. Building more than one home from the plans without permission is an infringement of the home designer's copyright. The purchase of a multiple-set package of plans is for the construction of a single home only. The purchase of additional sets of plans does not grant the right to construct more than one home.

4. HOUSE PLANS IN THE FORM OF BLUEPRINTS OR BLACKLINES CANNOT BE COPIED OR REPRODUCED

Plans, blueprints, or blacklines, unless they are reproducibles, cannot be copied or reproduced without prior written consent of the copyright owner. Copy shops and blueprinters are prohibited from making copies of these plans without the copyright release letter you receive with reproducible plans.

5. HOUSE PLANS IN THE FORM OF BLUEPRINTS OR BLACKLINES CANNOT BE REDRAWN

Plans cannot be modified or redrawn without first obtaining the copyright owner's permission. With your purchase of plans, you are licensed to make non-structural changes by "red-lining" the purchased plans. If you need to make structural changes or need to redraw the plans for any reason, you must purchase a reproducible set of plans (see topic 6) which includes a license to modify the plans. Blueprints do not come with a license to make structural changes or to redraw the plans. You may not reuse or sell the modified design.

6. REPRODUCIBILE HOME PLANS

Reproducible plans (for example sepias, mylars, CAD files, electronic files, and vellums) come with a license to make modifications to the plans. Once modified, the plans can be taken to a local copy shop or blueprinter to make up to 10 or 12 copies of the plans to use in the construction of a single home. Only one home can be constructed from any single purchased set of reproducible plans either in original form or as modified. The license to modify and copy must be completed and returned before the plan will be shipped.

7. MODIFIED DESIGNS CANNOT BE REUSED

Even if you are licensed to make modifications to a copyrighted design, the modified design is not free from the original designer's copyright. The sale or reuse of the modified design is prohibited. Also, be aware that any modification to plans relieves the original designer from liability for design defects and voids all warranties expressed or implied.

8. WHO IS RESPONSIBLE FOR COPYRIGHT INFRINGEMENT?

Any party who participates in a copyright violation may be responsible including the purchaser, designers, architects, engineers, drafters, homeowners, builders, contractors, sub-contractors, copy shops, blueprinters, developers, and real estate agencies. It does not matter whether or not the individual knows that a violation is being committed. Ignorance of the law is not a valid defense.

9. PLEASE RESPECT HOME DESIGN COPYRIGHTS

In the event of any suspected violation of a copyright, or if there is any uncertainty about the plans purchased, the publisher, architect, designer, or the Council of Publishing Home Designers (www.cphd.org) should be contacted before proceeding. Awards are sometimes offered for information about home design copyright infringement.

10. PENALTIES FOR INFRINGEMENT

Penalties for violating a copyright may be severe. The responsible parties are required to pay actual damages caused by the infringement (which may be substantial), plus any profits made by the infringer commissions to include all profits from the sale of any home built from an infringing design. The copyright law also allows for the recovery of statutory damages, which may be as high as $150,000 for each infringement. Finally, the infringer may be required to pay legal fees which often exceed the damages.

BLUEPRINT PRICE SCHEDULE

PRICE TIERS	1-SET STUDY PACKAGE	5-SET BUILDING PACKAGE	8-SET BUILDING PACKAGE	1-SET REPRODUCIBLE*
A1	$465	$515	$570	$695
A2	$505	$560	$615	$755
A3	$555	$625	$685	$845
A4	$610	$680	$745	$920
C1	$660	$735	$800	$980
C2	$710	$785	$845	$1,055
C3	$755	$835	$900	$1,135
C4	$810	$885	$955	$1,210
L1	$920	$1,020	$1,105	$1,375
L2	$1,000	$1,095	$1,185	$1,500
L3	$1,105	$1,210	$1,310	$1,650
L4	$1,220	$1,335	$1,425	$1,830
SQ1				.40/SQ. FT.
SQ3				.55/SQ. FT.
SQ5				.80/SQ. FT.

PRICES SUBJECT TO CHANGE

* REQUIRES A FAX NUMBER

PLAN #	PRICE TIER	PAGE	MATERIALS LIST	QUOTE ONE®	DECK	DECK PRICE	LANDSCAPE	LANDSCAPE PRICE	REGIONS
HPK1900001	C3	6	Y						
HPK1900002	C2	8	Y						
HPK1900003	C2	12							
HPK1900004	C2	13	Y	Y					
HPK1900005	C1	14	Y						
HPK1900006	C1	15	Y						
HPK1900007	C1	16	Y						
HPK1900008	C1	17	Y	Y					
HPK1900009	C1	18	Y						
HPK1900010	C1	19	Y						
HPK1900011	A3	20							
HPK1900012	A4	21							
HPK1900013	C1	22	Y						
HPK1900014	A3	23	Y						
HPK1900015	A2	24	Y						
HPK1900016	A3	25							
HPK1900017	A4	26							
HPK1900018	A2	27							
HPK1900019	A4	28							
HPK1900020	A4	29							
HPK1900021	A4	30							
HPK1900022	A4	31							
HPK1900023	A4	32	Y						
HPK1900024	A4	33							
HPK1900025	C2	34							
HPK1900026	C2	35							
HPK1900027	C2	36							
HPK1900028	C3	37							
HPK1900029	C2	38							
HPK1900030	C1	39							

PLAN #	PRICE TIER	PAGE	MATERIALS LIST	QUOTE ONE®	DECK	DECK PRICE	LANDSCAPE	LANDSCAPE PRICE	REGIONS
HPK1900031	C1	40							
HPK1900032	C2	41							
HPK1900033	C2	42							
HPK1900034	C1	43							
HPK1900035	A3	44							
HPK1900036	C2	45							
HPK1900037	SQ1	46	Y						
HPK1900038	C1	47							
HPK1900039	A3	48	Y	Y			OLA091	P3	12345678
HPK1900040	A4	49	Y						
HPK1900041	A4	50	Y						
HPK1900042	C1	51	Y						
HPK1900043	C2	52	Y						
HPK1900044	C2	53	Y						
HPK1900045	C1	54							
HPK1900046	A3	55	Y						
HPK1900047	A4	56	Y						
HPK1900048	A3	57							
HPK1900049	C1	58							
HPK1900050	A4	59							
HPK1900051	A4	60							
HPK1900052	A4	61							
HPK1900053	C1	62							
HPK1900054	C1	63							
HPK1900055	C1	64	Y						
HPK1900056	C2	65							
HPK1900057	A2	66							
HPK1900058	A2	67							
HPK1900059	A4	68	Y	Y	ODA012	P3	OLA083	P3	12345678
HPK1900060	C2	69	Y						

ORDER BLUEPRINTS 24 HOURS, 7 DAYS A WEEK, AT 1-800-521-6797

hanley▲wood

PLAN #	PRICE TIER	PAGE	MATERIALS LIST	QUOTE ONE®	DECK	DECK PRICE	LANDSCAPE	LANDSCAPE PRICE	REGIONS
HPK1900061	C1	70	Y						
HPK1900062	C2	71	Y						
HPK1900063	C3	72	Y	Y					
HPK1900064	C2	73	Y						
HPK1900065	C2	74	Y	Y					
HPK1900066	C2	75	Y						
HPK1900067	C3	76							
HPK1900068	C1	78	Y						
HPK1900069	SQ1	79							
HPK1900070	SQ1	80	Y						
HPK1900071	C1	81							
HPK1900072	SQ1	82							
HPK1900073	C1	83							
HPK1900074	SQ1	84	Y	Y			OLA010	P3	1234568
HPK1900075	A4	85							
HPK1900076	SQ1	86							
HPK1900077	C1	87	Y						
HPK1900078	C1	88							
HPK1900079	A4	89							
HPK1900080	C4	90	Y						
HPK1900081	A3	91	Y						
HPK1900082	C2	92	Y						
HPK1900083	A2	93	Y						
HPK1900084	A3	94	Y						
HPK1900085	A3	95	Y						
HPK1900086	A3	96	Y						
HPK1900087	A3	97	Y						
HPK1900088	A2	98	Y						
HPK1900089	A3	99	Y						
HPK1900090	A3	100	Y						
HPK1900091	A4	101	Y						
HPK1900092	A3	102	Y						
HPK1900093	A3	103	Y						
HPK1900094	C1	104							
HPK1900095	A4	105							
HPK1900096	C2	106							
HPK1900097	C2	107							
HPK1900098	SQ1	108							
HPK1900099	C4	109							
HPK1900100	C2	110	Y						
HPK1900101	A3	111							
HPK1900102	A3	112							
HPK1900103	A3	113	Y						
HPK1900104	A3	114	Y						
HPK1900105	A3	115							
HPK1900106	A3	116	Y						
HPK1900107	C3	117							
HPK1900108	A4	118							
HPK1900109	C1	119							
HPK1900110	C2	120							
HPK1900111	A3	121							
HPK1900112	C1	122							
HPK1900113	A4	123							
HPK1900114	C2	124							
HPK1900115	A2	125							
HPK1900116	A3	126							

PLAN #	PRICE TIER	PAGE	MATERIALS LIST	QUOTE ONE®	DECK	DECK PRICE	LANDSCAPE	LANDSCAPE PRICE	REGIONS
HPK1900117	C2	127	Y						
HPK1900118	C1	128							
HPK1900119	C1	129							
HPK1900120	A4	130	Y						
HPK1900121	C1	131	Y						
HPK1900122	A3	132	Y						
HPK1900123	A2	133	Y						
HPK1900124	A4	134	Y						
HPK1900125	C1	135	Y						
HPK1900126	C1	136	Y						
HPK1900127	C3	137	Y						
HPK1900128	C2	138	Y						
HPK1900129	A3	139	Y	Y	ODA011	P2	OLA093	P3	12345678
HPK1900130	A4	140	Y	Y					
HPK1900131	C2	141	Y	Y	ODA012	P3	OLA024	P4	123568
HPK1900132	SQ1	142	Y		ODA011	P2	OLA088	P4	12345678
HPK1900133	C3	143							
HPK1900134	C1	144							
HPK1900135	A3	145							
HPK1900136	A4	146							
HPK1900137	C3	147							
HPK1900138	C1	148							
HPK1900139	C1	149							
HPK1900140	C2	150							
HPK1900141	C2	151							
HPK1900142	C4	152							
HPK1900143	C3	153							
HPK1900144	SQ1	154	Y	Y					
HPK1900145	C4	156							
HPK1900146	A4	157							
HPK1900147	SQ1	158							
HPK1900148	SQ1	159							
HPK1900149	SQ3	160							
HPK1900150	C4	161	Y						
HPK1900151	L4	162							
HPK1900152	C3	163							
HPK1900153	C1	164							
HPK1900154	C2	165							
HPK1900155	A4	166	Y						
HPK1900156	C1	167	Y						
HPK1900157	A4	168	Y						
HPK1900158	C3	169	Y	Y			OLA024	P4	123568
HPK1900159	C4	170							
HPK1900160	L1	171	Y						
HPK1900161	C3	172							
HPK1900162	SQ3	173							
HPK1900163	L1	174							
HPK1900164	C3	175	Y	Y					
HPK1900165	L1	176							
HPK1900166	SQ1	177							
HPK1900167	C3	178							
HPK1900168	L2	179							
HPK1900169	L2	180	Y						
HPK1900170	C3	181							

A successful farmhouse design knows
its history and invokes a common
desire for simple, honest living. See
more of this home on page 78.